As per Revised Syllabus under CBCGS System of BMS Course under Mumbai University w.e.f. June, 2018.

CUSTOMER RELATIONSHIP MANAGEMENT

(BMS Third Year: Fifth Semester)
(Marketing Group – Elective)

Dr. Rashmi
(Ph.D. M.Com, B.ed

First Edition

Preface

It is with immense joy and a sense of accomplishment that I present this book, "Customer Relationship Management," tailored specifically for the TYBMS curriculum of Mumbai University. This endeavor has been a labor of love, and I am grateful for the opportunity to contribute to the academic journey of BMS students.

The decision to write a book on Customer Relationship Management (CRM) was driven by a deep-seated belief in the transformative power of effective customer engagement. In today's dynamic business landscape, where relationships form the cornerstone of success, understanding and mastering the principles of CRM is more critical than ever. This book seeks to demystify the intricacies of CRM, providing students with a comprehensive and practical guide to navigate this pivotal aspect of business management.

The creation of this book has been a collaborative effort, and I extend my deepest gratitude to my family for their unwavering support and understanding throughout this journey. To my husband, CA Neeraj Kumar, whose encouragement and expertise have been a guiding light, I owe a debt of gratitude. His insights and invaluable suggestions have enriched the content and elevated the quality of this work.

To my children, Jivitesh Aggarwal and Jayant Aggarwal, your patience and understanding during the long hours devoted to this project have been truly remarkable. Your love and encouragement have been my inspiration, and I dedicate this book to you with all my heart.

I would also like to express my sincere appreciation to [Publisher's Name], the esteemed publisher who recognized the merit of this work and provided the platform to bring it to fruition. The collaboration with [Publisher's Name] has been instrumental in shaping this book into its final form, and I am grateful for the opportunity to be part of your distinguished publishing house.

To the readers, educators, and students who embark on this learning journey with "Customer Relationship Management," I hope you find the content insightful, accessible, and beneficial to your academic pursuits.

Thank you to everyone who has played a role, big or small, in making this project a reality. Your support has been the cornerstone of this endeavor, and for that, I am truly thankful.

With warm regards,

Dr. Rashmi

Syllabus

Customer Relationship Management

Objectives
1. To understand concept of Customer Relationship Management (CRM) and implementation of Customer Relationship Management
2. To provide insight into CRM marketing initiatives, customer service and designing CRM strategy
3. To understand new trends in CRM, challenges and opportunities for organizations

SN	Modules/Units
1	**Introduction to Customer Relationship Management**
	- Concept, Evolution of Customer Relationships: Customers as strangers, acquaintances, friends and partners - Objectives, Benefits of CRM to Customers and Organisations, Customer Profitability Segments, Components of CRM: Information, Process, Technology and People, Barriers to CRM - Relationship Marketing and CM: Relationship Development Strategies: Organizational Pervasive Approach, Managing Customer Emotions, Brand Building through Relationship Marketing, Service Level Agreements, Relationship Challenges
2	**CRM Marketing Initiatives, Customer Service and Data Management**
	- CRM Marketing Initiatives: Cross-Selling and Up-Selling, Customer Retention, Behaviour Prediction, Customer Profitability and Value Modeling, Channel Optimization, Personalization and Event-Based Marketing - CRM and Customer Service: Call Center and Customer Care: Call Routing, Contact Center Sales-Support, Web Based Self Service, Customer Satisfaction Measurement, Call-Scripting, Cyber Agents and Workforce Management - CRM and Data Management: Types of Data: Reference Data, Transactional Data, Warehouse Data and Business View Data, Identifying Data Quality Issues, Planning and Getting Information Quality, Using Tools to Manage Data, Types of Data Analysis: Online Analytical Processing (OLAP), Clickstream Analysis, Personalisation and Collaborative Filtering, Data Reporting
3	**CRM Strategy, Planning, Implementation and Evaluation**
	- Understanding Customers: Customer Value, Customer Care, Company Profit Chain: Satisfaction, Loyalty, Retention and Profits - Objectives of CRM Strategy, The CRM Strategy Cycle: Acquisition, Retention and Win Back, Complexities of CRM Strategy - Planning and Implementation of CRM: Business to Business CRM, Sales and CRM, Sales Force Automation, Sales Process/ Activity Management, Sales Territory Management, Contact Management, Lead Management, Configuration Support, Knowledge Management CRM Implementation: Steps- Business Planning, Architecture and Design, Technology Selection, Development, Delivery and Measurement - CRM Evaluation: Basic Measures: Service Quality, Customer Satisfaction and Loyalty, Company 3E Measures: Efficiency, Effectiveness and Employee Change
4	**CRM New Horizons**
	- e-CRM: Concept, Different Levels of E- CRM, Privacy in E-CRM - Software App for Customer Service:

- Activity Management, Agent Management, Case Assignment, Contract Management, Customer Self Service, Email Response Management, Escalation, Inbound Communication Management, Invoicing, Outbound Communication Management, Queuing and Routing, Scheduling
- Social Networking and CRM
- Mobile-CRM
- CRM Trends, Challenges and Opportunities
- Ethical Issues in CRM

CONTENTS

No.	Modules/Units	Pages
1.	Introduction to Customer Relationship Management	
2.	CRM Marketing Initiatives, Customer Service and Data Management	
3.	CRM Strategy, Planning, Implementation and Evaluation	
4.	CRM New Horizons	

UNIT 1

INTRODUCTION TO CUSTOMER RELATIONSHIP MANAGEMENT

- ✓ Concept of customer relationship management
- ✓ Introduction to customer
- ✓ Categories of customer:
- ✓ Evolution of customer relationships
- ✓ Objectives of customer relationship management
- ✓ Benefits of CRM
- ✓ Disadvantages of CRM
- ✓ Types of CRM
- ✓ Segmentation of customers as per profitability
- ✓ Components of customer relationship management
- ✓ Barriers to customer relationship
- ✓ Relationship marketing
- ✓ Difference between relationship marketing and customer relationship management
- ✓ Relationship development strategies
- ✓ Organisational pervasive approach
- ✓ Managing customers emotions
- ✓ Brand building through relationship marketing
- ✓ Service level agreements
- ✓ Relationship challenges
- ✓ Questions

CONCEPT OF CUSTOMER RELATIONSHIP MANAGEMENT (April, 2023; Nov. 2019; April, 2019)

Customer Relationship Management (CRM) is a strategic approach that businesses use to manage and analyze customer interactions throughout the customer lifecycle. The goal of CRM is to improve customer relationships, drive customer retention, and enhance overall profitability.

In simple words, Customer Relationship Management, or CRM, is like having a personal memory aid for a business. Imagine you have a friend who remembers everything about your likes, dislikes, and your past conversations. In a similar way, CRM is a tool that helps businesses remember and manage information about their customers.

For example, let's say you have a favorite coffee shop. The barista remembers your name, your usual order, and that you prefer your coffee with a little extra cream. That's a bit like what CRM does for businesses but on a larger scale. It helps companies keep track of customer details, interactions, and preferences so they can provide better and more personalized services.

Customer relationship management is comprised of three words:

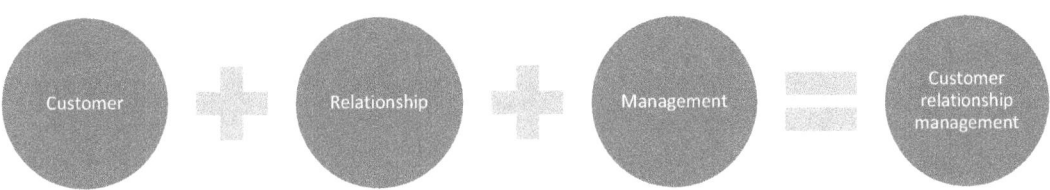

Customer: This is the person who buys things or uses services from a store or a company. It's like when you go to a candy store and buy your favorite sweets. The store wants to know what you like so they can make you happy.

Relationship: This is about being friends with the people who come to the store. Imagine if the candy store owner remembers your name, knows your favorite candies, and always has a friendly chat with you. That makes you feel good, right? Building a relationship is like making the store a friendly place where customers want to come back.

Management: This is like being really organized. The store needs to keep track of what candies are popular, when they need to order more, and who their regular customers are. It's like having a plan to make sure everything runs smoothly, just like when you plan how to organize your toys or games.

INTRODUCTION TO CUSTOMER

A customer is an individual, organization, or entity that purchases goods or services from a business or engages in some form of transaction with a provider. Customers are essential to the success of any business, as they represent the primary source of revenue and feedback.

Types of customer:

There are two types of customer: Internal and external customer

Internal Customer:

An internal customer refers to individuals or departments within the same organization who rely on the products, services, or support of another department or individual within the organization. In essence, internal customers are employees or units that interact as service providers and recipients within the same company. For example, in a manufacturing company, the production department might be considered an internal customer of the procurement department, as it depends on the timely delivery of raw materials.

External Customer:

An external customer is an individual, organization, or entity outside the boundaries of the company that purchases goods, services, or products from the business. External customers are the end-users of the products or services offered by the organization. For instance, in a retail setting, the people buying the products from the store are considered external customers.

Categories of customer:

There are four types of consumer:

Undaunted Striver

Savvy Maximiser

Content Streamer

Secure Traditionalists

Undaunted Striver:

These types of customers are also known as loyal and technology-driven customer. These customers are most trend oriented and product-focussed. They are ambitious, risk-taking, and determined individuals who actively seek challenges to achieve their goals. They are likely to embrace innovation and are not afraid to step out of their comfort zones.

In other words, they have "child" like personality.

For example, think of a friend who always wants to use the latest gadgets and apps on their phone. They enjoy being the first to try new games or tools. This friend is not afraid to learn and do new things, just like a child who is always curious and eager to discover.

Savvy Maximiser:

These types of customers are also known as bargain hunter. These customers are really good at getting the most out of their money. They love finding deals and making sure they save as much as possible. They're the "smart spenders." Discount attracts them to a great extent. A good bargain hunter seeks to beat the seller down, no matter how good the deal. They will keep asking for more until they are certain they will not get more.

For example, think of someone who always looks for discounts and coupons when shopping, like a friend who knows all the best sales and never pays full price.

Content Streamer:

These types of customers are also known as judgemental customer. This type of customer is suspicious of everyone, believing that all people are selfish. They will never believe what the seller says. After all, he is trying to sell to them and therefore will deceive them. A judgmental customer is someone who forms opinions or evaluations about products, services, or people based on their own standards or biases. This customer may be quick to make decisions or assessments and may have strong preferences. Here's a simple example to illustrate a judgmental customer:

For example, imagine a person walks into a new restaurant and looks around. Without even trying the food, they quickly decide whether they like it or not based on the décor, the appearance of the staff, or their initial impression. If the person decides that the restaurant doesn't meet their specific expectations, they might leave without giving the food a chance. In this case, the customer is making judgments about the restaurant based on limited information and personal biases.

Secure Traditionalists:

These types of customers are also known as matured customers. Such type of customers knows just what they want and do not want to try any other goods or services. They will not negotiate. They will tell the seller what they want and expect them to give at the best price. They approach purchases and interactions with a sense of experience, wisdom, and consideration. Matured customers often make decisions based on a thorough evaluation of products or services, and they may prioritize long-term value and quality. Here's a simple example to illustrate a matured customer:

For example, consider a person who is in the market for a new smartphone. A matured customer might research different models, read reviews, and compare features to understand which phone best meets their needs. Instead of being swayed by flashy advertisements or the latest trends, they prioritize factors like reliability, battery life, and overall performance.

When making the purchase, the matured customer may consider the brand's reputation for producing durable products and choose a phone that aligns with their practical needs. This customer values informed decision-making and tends to invest in products that offer lasting value rather than being influenced by short-term trends.

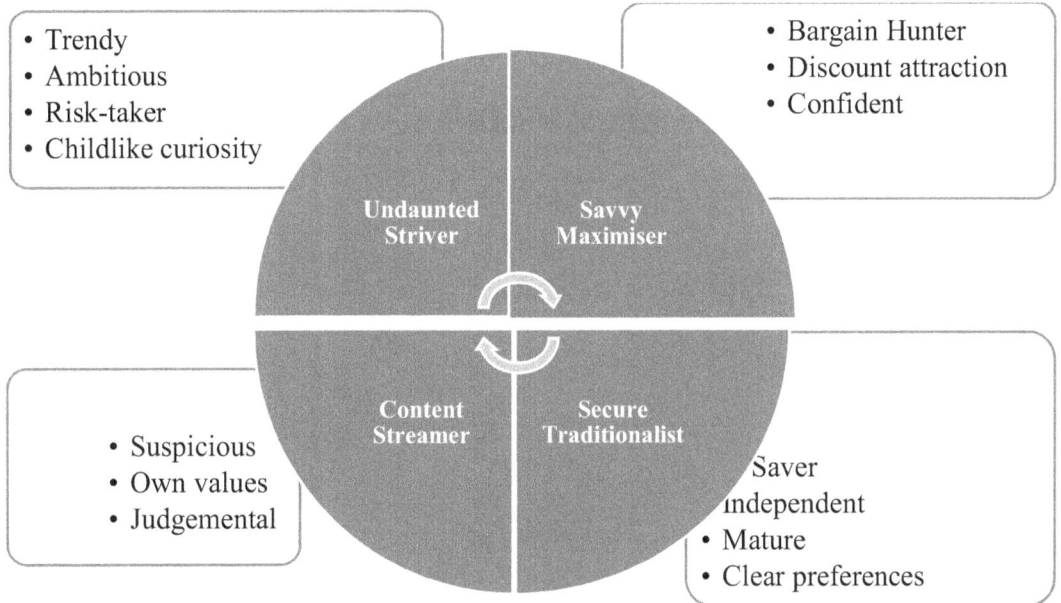

EVOLUTION OF CUSTOMER RELATIONSHIPS: CUSTOMER AS STRANGERS, AQUAINTERS, FRIENDS AND PARTNERS (April, 2023; Nov. 2019; April, 2019)

The evolution of customer relationships can be understood in stages: from viewing customers as strangers to cultivating partnerships. Let's explore each stage with examples:

Customers as Strangers:

At the beginning, customers are essentially strangers to the business. There's no prior interaction, and the business has limited knowledge about their preferences or needs. For example, imagine a person walking into a new retail store for the first time. The store has no information about the customer, and the interaction is transactional.

Customers as Acquaintances:

As customers make repeat visits or transactions, the relationship evolves. The business starts to recognize them and gathers basic information about their preferences. For example, the same person starts becoming a regular customer at the store. The staff begins to recognize them and may offer general recommendations based on their previous purchases.

Customers as Friends:

In this stage, the business establishes a more personalized and friendly relationship with the customer. There's a deeper understanding of their preferences, and efforts are made to enhance their experience. For example, the store, recognizing the customer's preferences, starts sending personalized discounts or offers. The staff may engage in friendly conversations, making the customer feel valued.

Customers as Partners:

At the partnership stage, the relationship becomes collaborative. The business and the customer work together towards mutual benefit. There's a high level of trust, and the business actively seeks customer feedback for improvement. For example, a tech company collaborates with a long-term client to co-create a customized solution that meets the client's specific needs. The partnership involves ongoing communication, joint planning, and a shared commitment to success.

OBJECTIVES OF CUSTOMER RELATIONSHIP MANAGEMENT (Nov. 2022; April, 2019)

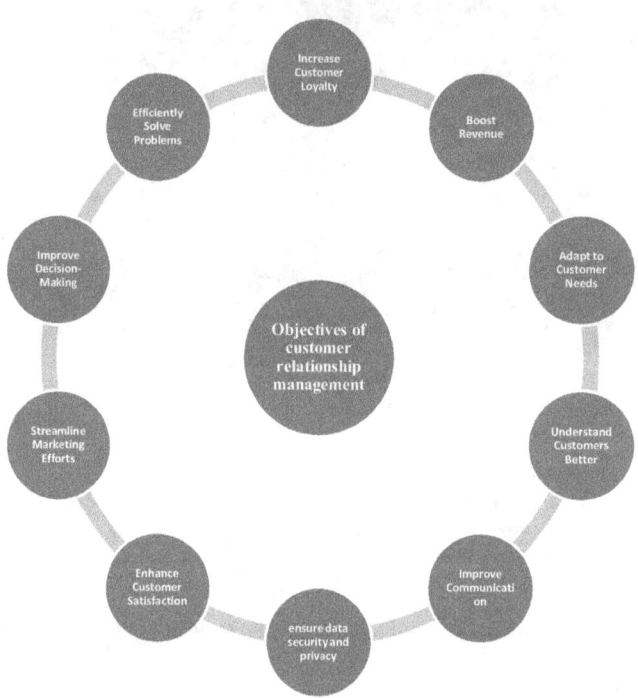

1. **Understand Customers Better**:
   With the help of CRM, businesses can know what customers like and want. For example, a coffee shop notices people prefer more iced drinks in the summer, so they make more of those.
2. **Improve Communication**:
   It helps to talk to customers in ways that make them happy. For example, an online store sends emails about sales on products customers are interested in.
3. **Efficiently Solve Problems**:

CRM helps in fixing issues quickly and keep customers satisfied. For example, a phone company knows your problem before you finish explaining it, making the solution faster.

4. **Increase Customer Loyalty**:
CRM aims at keep customers coming back and don't go to other businesses. For example, a restaurant remembers your favorite dish, making you want to go there again.

5. **Boost Revenue**:
CRM is used to make more money by selling things customers really like. For example, an app introduces a new feature people love, so more people buy it, bringing in more money.

6. **Adapt to Customer Needs**:
CRM guides the business to change and improve itself based on what customers like. For example, a streaming service adds a feature customer have been asking for, making them happy and more likely to keep using it.

7. **Ensure Data Security and Privacy**:
CRM keep customer information safe and only use it to make their experience better. For example, an online store has secure accounts, and they only send updates that customers want, respecting their privacy.

8. **Enhance Customer Satisfaction**:
The purpose of CRM is to make customers feel happy and satisfied with the overall experience. For example, a hotel remembers your room preferences, making your stay comfortable and enjoyable.

9. **Streamline Marketing Efforts**:
CRM saves time and money by promoting products to the right people. For example, a fashion store sends promotions for specific styles to customers who have shown interest in those styles.

10. **Improve Decision-Making**:
With the help of CRM, business makes better choices based on information about what customers like. For example, a company decides to launch a new product after considering customer feedback, increasing the chances of success.

BENEFITS OF CRM (Nov. 2022)

Benefits of CRM can be discussed under three heads:

- Benefits to Customers
- Benefits to Organisation
- Other benefits

Customer Relationship Management

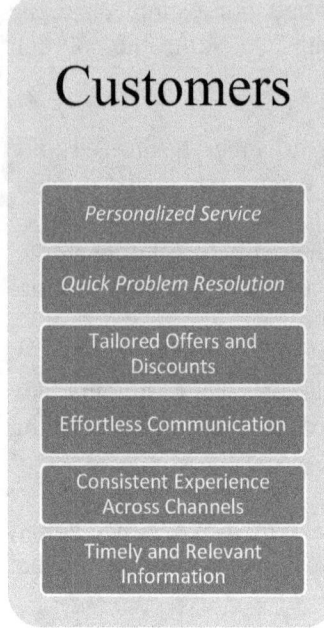
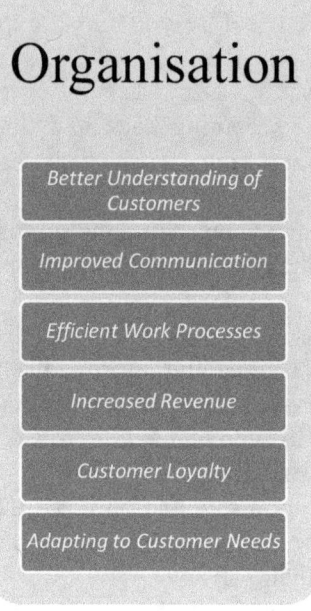
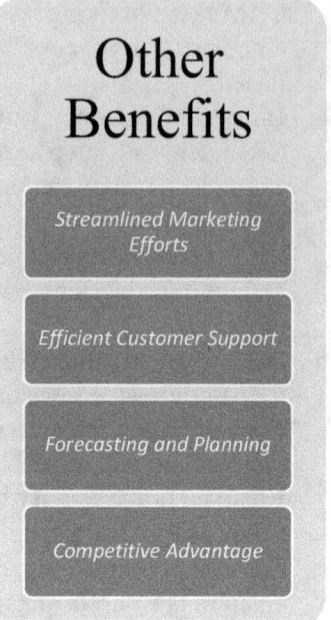

Benefits of CRM to the customers:

1. *Personalized Service*:
   Businesses can remember what you like and give you a more personalized experience. For example, when you visit your favorite coffee shop, and they already know how you like your coffee without asking every time.
2. *Quick Problem Resolution:*
   If there's an issue with something you bought, they can fix it faster because they have all your information. For example, when you call a customer service hotline, and they quickly solve your problem because they know your purchase history.
3. Tailored Offers and Discounts:
   Businesses can give you special deals and discounts based on what you like. For example, getting a discount on your favorite brand of shoes because the store knows you buy them often.
4. Effortless Communication:
   Companies can easily let you know about new products or updates. For example, receiving an email about a sale on items you've shown interest in or bought before.
5. Consistent Experience Across Channels:
   Whether you're on their website, app, or in-store, they treat you the same way. For example, your favorite online store remembering your preferences when you visit their physical store.
6. Timely and Relevant Information:
   They can tell you about things that matter to you at the right time. For example, getting a notification about a concert of your favorite band in your city because the ticketing app knows your music preferences.

Benefits of CRM to the organisation:

1. *Better Understanding of Customers*:

Companies can learn more about what their customers like and want. For example, a store realizes that most customers prefer a specific type of shoe, so they stock more of that kind.
2. *Improved Communication*:
Businesses can talk to customers in ways that make them happy. For example, a company sends you emails about products you might like based on your past purchases.
3. *Efficient Work Processes*:
Employees can do their jobs faster and better because everything they need is organized. For example, when you call customer service, they quickly find your information, making the conversation smoother.
4. *Increased Revenue*:
Companies can make more money by selling things that customers really want. For example, a music streaming service introduces a new feature that customers love, so more people subscribe, bringing in more money.
5. *Customer Loyalty*:
Customers keep coming back because they like the company. For example, a restaurant remembers your favorite dish, and you keep going there because they make you feel special.
6. *Adapting to Customer Needs*:
Businesses can change and improve based on what customers like and don't like. For example, a software company updates its app with features customers have been asking for, making them happier and more likely to keep using it.

Other Benefits:

1. *Streamlined Marketing Efforts*:
Companies can save time and money by promoting products to the right people. For example, an online store sends promotions for sports gear to customers who have previously bought sports-related items.
2. *Efficient Customer Support*:
When you have a problem, businesses can solve it quickly because they know your history. For example, calling a tech support line, and they already know what products you have and can help you faster.
3. *Forecasting and Planning*:
Businesses can predict future trends and plan for what customers might want. For example, a clothing store orders more winter jackets before the season starts because they know it's a popular item.
4. *Competitive Advantage*:
Companies can be better than others because they understand and serve customers better. For example, a bookstore offers personalized book recommendations, standing out from other generic bookstores.

DISADVANTAGES OF CRM

Customer Relationship Management

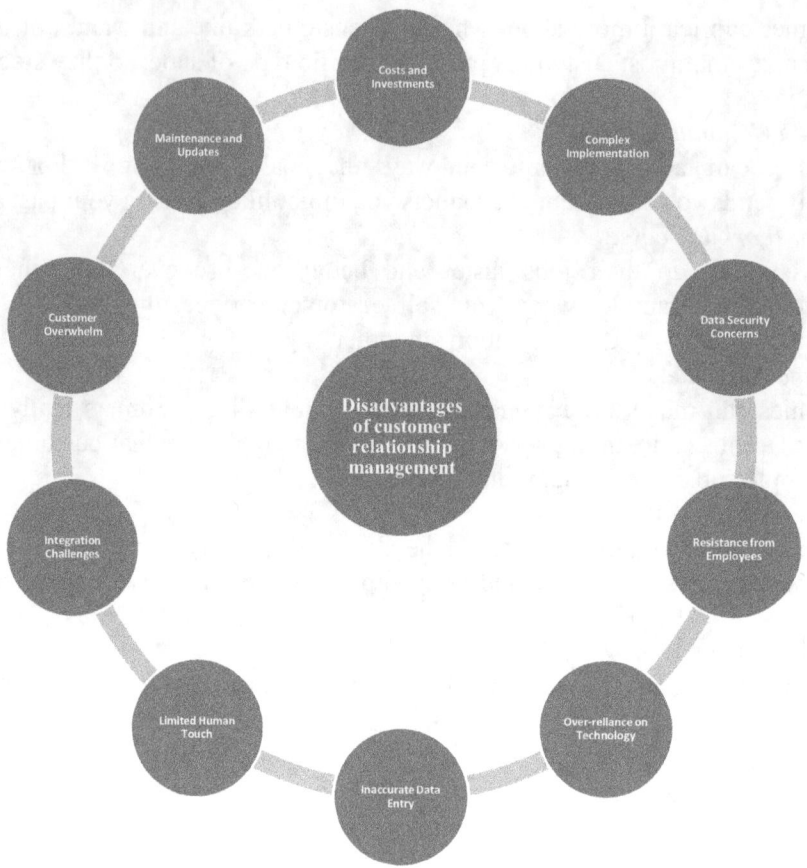

1. **Costs and Investments:**
   Setting up and maintaining a CRM system can be expensive for businesses. For example, a small local store might find it hard to afford a fancy CRM system, affecting their budget.
2. **Complex Implementation:**
   Installing and using CRM systems can be complicated and take time to learn. For example, employees at a small bakery might find it challenging to use a complex CRM software, slowing down their work.
3. **Data Security Concerns:**
   Storing customer information can lead to worries about data breaches and privacy issues. For example, if a company's database gets hacked, customer details like emails or addresses might be exposed.
4. **Resistance from Employees:**
   Employees might resist using CRM systems, feeling it adds extra work. For example, staff at a local bookstore might prefer their old manual system and resist using a new digital CRM tool.
5. **Over-reliance on Technology:**
   Relying too much on CRM technology might make businesses neglect personal interactions with customers. For example, a restaurant using CRM might forget the importance of a friendly chat with regular customers.
6. **Inaccurate Data Entry:**
   If employees enter wrong information into the CRM system, it can lead to mistakes. For example, a typing error in a customer's email address could result in them not getting important updates.
7. **Limited Human Touch:**

Excessive use of CRM might make interactions feel robotic, lacking the warmth of human connections. For example, a customer might miss the personal touch of a handwritten thank-you note instead of an automated email.

8. **Integration Challenges**:
Integrating CRM with other business systems can be challenging and cause disruptions. For example, a bakery might face difficulties connecting their CRM system with the inventory management software, causing issues with stock tracking.

9. **Customer Overwhelm**:
Bombarding customers with too much personalized information can be overwhelming. For example, getting daily emails from a store might annoy a customer rather than make them feel special.

10. **Maintenance and Updates**:
Regular maintenance and updates are required, and businesses may struggle to keep up. For example, a small online shop might face difficulties updating its CRM software regularly due to limited resources.

TYPES OF CRM (Nov. 2022)

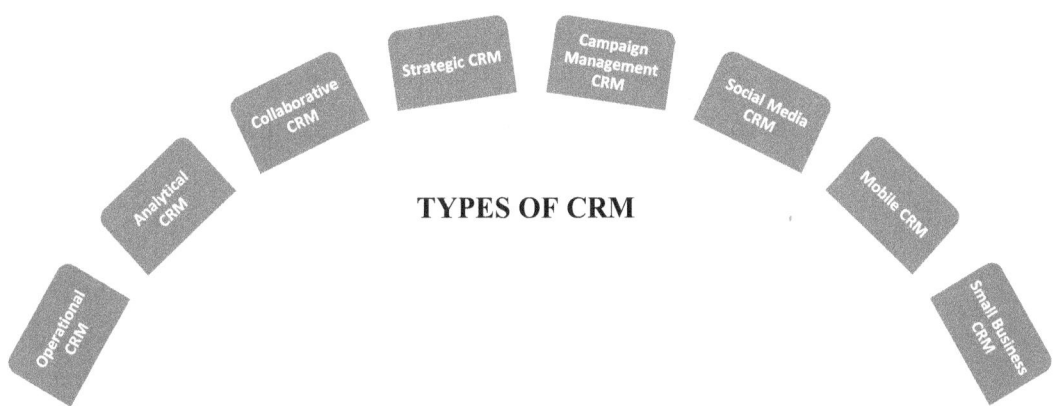

1. **Operational CRM**:
This type focuses on the day-to-day interactions with customers, like sales, marketing, and service. For example, when you call a customer service hotline, and they quickly find your information to help you with a problem.

2. **Analytical CRM**:
Analytical CRM uses data and analytics to understand customer behavior and improve business strategies. For example, an online store analyzes which products are popular to plan what to stock more of in the future.

3. **Collaborative CRM**:
Collaborative CRM is about sharing customer information across different departments to provide better service. For example, when the sales team and customer service team share notes about a customer to give a more personalized experience.

4. **Strategic CRM**:
Strategic CRM focuses on long-term goals and how to keep customers happy over time. For example, a hotel planning to introduce new services based on what customers have been asking for.

5. **Campaign Management CRM**:

This type of CRM helps in plan and execute marketing campaigns to reach and attract customers. For example, sending out special offers through emails to customers who haven't shopped in a while.

6. **Social Media CRM**:
Social Media CRM involves managing and engaging with customers through social platforms. For example, responding to customer queries or comments on social media to maintain a positive online presence.

7. **Mobile CRM**
Mobile CRM allows businesses to interact with customers through mobile devices. For example, using a mobile app to make reservations at a restaurant or track a package delivery.

8. **Small Business CRM**:
This is a simplified CRM version designed for small businesses with fewer resources. For example, a local bakery using a simple CRM tool to keep track of customer preferences and order history.

SEGMENTATION OF CUSTOMERS AS PER PROFITABILITY (April, 2019; Nov. 2018)

Customer Relationship Management (CRM) involves categorizing customers based on their value to the business, allowing companies to tailor their strategies and efforts accordingly.

Customers are classified into categories based on their profitability to the organization.

	Profitable Customers	Unprofitable customers
Profitable products	BEST CUSTOMERS (Quadrant I)	PROFIT POTENTIAL CUSTOMERS (Quadrant II)
Unprofitable products	SLOW LEAK CUSTOMERS (Quadrant III)	WORST CUSTOMERS (Quadrant IV)

Quadrant I (Best Customers):

These are the customers who really love our products or services and buy from us a lot. For example, imagine people who always shop at our store and tell their friends about us. They are our best customers.

Characteristics:

- High-frequency and high-value transactions.
- Demonstrated loyalty over an extended period.
- Positive interactions and feedback.

Strategies:

- Loyalty programs to reinforce their commitment.
- Exclusive offers and personalized incentives.

Quadrant II (Profit Potential Customers):

These are customers who like us but could buy even more if we give them some special deals or show them more of what they might like. For example, think of someone who sometimes buys from us. If we give them a special offer, they might buy more things.

Characteristics:

- Moderate to high transaction frequency.
- Have shown an interest in additional products or services.
- May require personalized marketing or promotions to increase engagement.

Strategies:

- Develop personalized campaigns based on their potential needs and preferences.
- Encourage increased engagement through targeted communication and promotions.

Quadrant III (Slow Leak Customers):

These are customers who used to buy a lot but now buy less. We need to figure out why and try to make them like us again. For example, consider someone who used to come to our shop often but hasn't been coming lately. We want to find out why and make them want to shop with us again.

Characteristics:

- Decreased transaction frequency.
- Changes in purchasing behavior or preferences.
- Possible indicators of dissatisfaction or reduced loyalty.

Strategies:

- Find Out Why:
- Ask them what changed and why they don't buy as much.
- Make It Right:
- Fix any issues they have and make them want to come back.

Quadrant IV (Worst Customers):

These are customers who don't buy much, and it costs us more to keep them as customers than what they give us in return. For example, think of someone who rarely buys from us, and when they do, it's not much. It costs us more to keep them happy than we get from them.

Characteristics:

- Rare or minimal transactions.
- Minimal brand loyalty or repeat business.
- Potential for high maintenance costs without corresponding value.

Strategies:

Evaluate Cost-Benefit:

- Assess the cost of maintaining the relationship against the value received.
- Consider whether efforts should be redirected to more profitable segments.
- Develop strategies for a graceful exit from unprofitable customer relationships.

COMPONENTS OF CUSTOMER RELATIONSHIP MANAGEMENT (April, 2023; Nov. 2019; April, 2019)

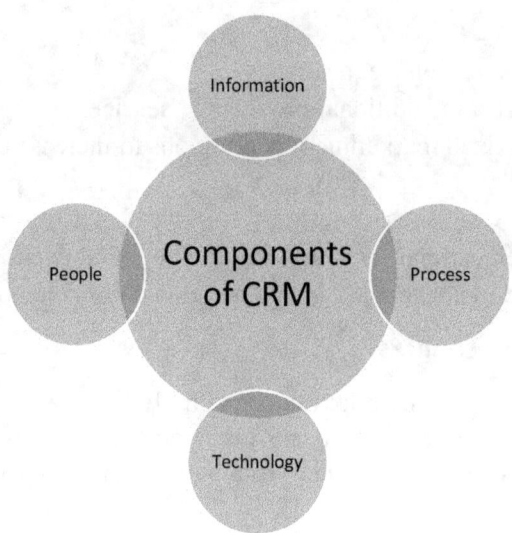

Information in CRM:

In CRM, information refers to the collection of data and details about customers. It's about understanding who are the customers, what are their preferences, behaviors, and interactions with the business. Customer information is crucial for tailoring your products or services to meet customer needs, improving customer satisfaction, and building long-lasting relationships. It allows you to anticipate customer expectations and deliver personalized experiences.

Types of Customer Information:

Basic Information: Includes customer names, contact details, and demographic data.

Transaction History: Details of past purchases, invoices, and payment history.

Preferences: Information about product preferences, communication channels, and buying habits.

Feedback and Reviews: Customer opinions, feedback, and reviews help in understanding satisfaction levels and areas for improvement.

Interactions: Records of customer interactions, such as emails, calls, and chat logs.

For example, imagine a local bookstore using CRM. They collect customer information like names, email addresses, and purchase history. With this information, they can recommend new books based on past purchases, send personalized promotions, and notify customers about book signings or events tailored to their interests.

Process in CRM:

In CRM, a process refers to the organized and structured series of steps and workflows that a company follows to manage its interactions with customers efficiently. It involves how customer-related tasks and activities are managed, tracked, and executed. CRM processes are vital for ensuring that customer interactions are consistent, well-coordinated, and aligned with business goals. They help streamline tasks, reduce errors, and enhance overall customer satisfaction.

Key Elements of CRM Processes:

Lead Management:

The process of tracking and managing potential customers (leads) from initial contact to conversion. For example, when a new lead is identified (e.g., through a website sign-up), the CRM process may involve assigning a sales representative, sending an introductory email, and scheduling follow-up calls.

Sales Pipeline:

The stages a customer goes through in the sales process, from initial contact to closing a deal. For example, a CRM process may include stages like lead qualification, product demonstration, negotiation, and closing the sale. Each stage involves specific actions and follow-ups.

Customer Support:

Managing and resolving customer inquiries, issues, or requests for assistance. For example, a CRM process for customer support may include ticket creation, assigning support agents, resolving issues, and following up to ensure customer satisfaction.

Marketing Campaigns:

Planning and executing marketing initiatives to reach and engage customers. For example, a CRM process for a marketing campaign might involve segmenting the customer base, creating targeted content, deploying the

Technology in CRM:

In CRM, technology refers to the use of software, tools, and systems to collect, organize, analyze, and manage customer information and interactions. It provides the infrastructure for implementing and supporting CRM processes.

Key Elements of CRM Technology:

CRM Software:

Specialized software designed to centralize customer data, automate processes, and facilitate communication with customers. For example, salesforce, HubSpot, and Zoho CRM are popular CRM software platforms that help businesses manage customer relationships effectively.

Database Management:

Systems that organize and store customer data in a structured manner for easy retrieval and analysis. For example, a database management system within CRM ensures that customer information is securely stored, easily accessible, and can be updated in real-time.

Automation Tools:

Tools that automate repetitive tasks and processes, saving time and reducing the risk of errors. For example, workflow automation in CRM can automatically trigger follow-up emails, assign tasks to team members, or update customer records based on predefined conditions.

Analytics and Reporting:

Tools that analyze customer data to provide insights, trends, and performance metrics. For example, CRM analytics can help businesses understand customer behavior, measure the success of marketing campaigns, and identify areas for improvement.

Integration Capabilities:

The ability of CRM systems to integrate with other business applications, such as email, marketing, and e-commerce platforms. For example, integration with email platforms allows CRM users to track and log email communications directly within the CRM system.

People:

The individuals in your company who use the information, follow the processes, and interact with customers directly.

Following are the different types of people in the organisation:

Customer-Facing Teams: These are the people who directly engage with customers. This includes sales representatives, customer service agents, and support staff. They use the CRM system to understand customer needs, preferences, and history.

Communication and Relationship Building: The "People" component emphasizes the human touch in customer interactions. It's about establishing relationships, understanding customer concerns, and providing personalized assistance.

Training and Adoption: Successful CRM implementation requires proper training for employees. The "People" aspect involves ensuring that your team is comfortable using the CRM tools effectively.

Collaboration: Different departments within a company often interact with the same customers. The CRM system encourages collaboration among employees, allowing them to share insights and coordinate efforts for a unified customer experience.

Adaptability: The "People" aspect also involves being adaptable to changing customer needs. Staff should be open to using new tools and approaches facilitated by the CRM system to enhance customer satisfaction.

For example, imagine a salesperson, Sarah, using the CRM system. She can see that a customer, John, has previously purchased a laptop. This knowledge helps Sarah recommend compatible accessories during John's next visit, creating a more personalized and satisfying experience for him. Additionally, the customer support team, armed with information from the CRM system, can provide faster and more accurate solutions to any issues John might encounter with his laptop.

BARRIERS TO CUSTOMER RELATIONSHIP MANAGEMENT (April, 2023; Nov. 2019; Nov. 2018)

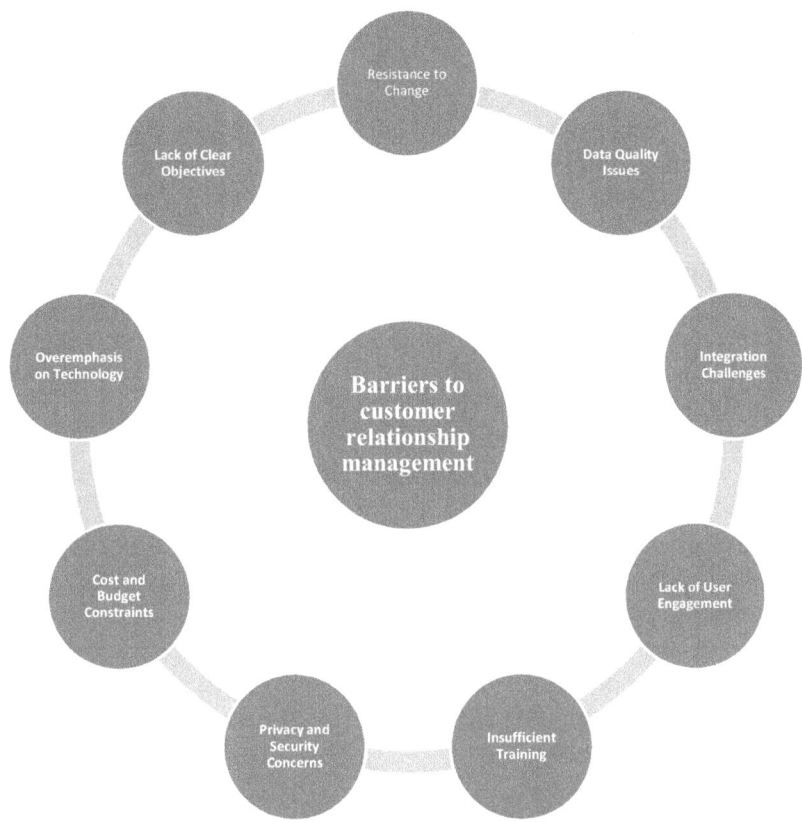

1. **Resistance to Change**:
   Employees or management may resist adopting new CRM systems and processes due to fear of change or unfamiliarity. For example, a company introduces a CRM system to streamline customer interactions. However, employees, accustomed to their existing methods, may resist using the new system, hindering its effectiveness.
2. **Data Quality Issues:**
   Inaccurate or incomplete data in the CRM system can lead to poor decision-making and unreliable customer insights. For example, if customer information is outdated or entered incorrectly, the CRM might suggest ineffective marketing strategies or result in misinformed customer interactions.
3. **Integration Challenges**:
   Difficulty integrating CRM with existing systems or other software applications within the organization. For example, a company uses separate tools for sales, marketing, and customer support. If these tools don't integrate seamlessly with the CRM system, it can lead to disjointed processes and information silos.
4. **Lack of User Engagement**:
   Employees may not fully engage with the CRM system, leading to underutilization and decreased effectiveness. For example, even if a company invests in a powerful CRM tool, if employees don't see the value or understand how to use it, they may revert to their previous, less efficient methods.
5. **Insufficient Training**:
   Inadequate training on how to use the CRM system can result in low user adoption rates and suboptimal utilization. For example, employees may struggle to navigate the CRM

interface, leading to frustration and the potential abandonment of the system in favor of familiar but less efficient processes.

6. **Privacy and Security Concerns**:
Concerns about the security and privacy of customer data can hinder CRM adoption. For example, if customers perceive that their personal information is not adequately protected within the CRM system, they may be hesitant to engage with the company or provide accurate data.

7. **Costs and Budget Constraints**:
The initial investment and ongoing costs associated with implementing and maintaining CRM systems can be a barrier, especially for smaller businesses. For example, a small business might find it challenging to allocate sufficient funds for a comprehensive CRM solution, limiting its ability to leverage advanced features.

8. **Overemphasis on Technology**:
Focusing too much on technology and neglecting the human and process aspects of CRM. For example, a company invests heavily in a sophisticated CRM tool but fails to align it with the existing processes and train employees effectively, resulting in underutilization and inefficiencies.

9. **Lack of Clear Objectives**:
Not having well-defined goals and objectives for CRM implementation can lead to confusion and a lack of direction. For example, a company adopts CRM without a clear understanding of what it aims to achieve, resulting in scattered efforts and minimal impact on customer relationships.

RELATIONSHIP MARKETING (April, 2023; Nov. 2018)

Relationship Marketing is a long-term strategy that emphasizes building and nurturing lasting relationships with customers rather than focusing solely on individual transactions. For examples, a coffee shop offering a loyalty program where customers earn points for every purchase, leading to discounts or free items. An online retailer sending personalized recommendations based on a customer's purchase history.

Principles of Relationship Marketing

Customer-Centric Approach: Prioritizes understanding and meeting the unique needs of individual customers.

Two-Way Communication: Encourages open and ongoing communication between the business and its customers.

Mutual Value Creation: Aims to create value for both the customer and the business over time.

Customer Loyalty: Focuses on cultivating customer loyalty and repeat business.

DIFFERENCE BETWEEN RELATIONSHIP MARKETING AND CUSTOMER RELATIONSHIP MANAGEMENT

Basis	RELATIONSHIP MARKETING	CUSTOMER RELATIONSHIP MANAGEMENT

Definition	It is a long-term strategy that emphasizes developing strong, mutually beneficial relationships with customers over time.	It is a comprehensive strategy that involves the systematic management of customer interactions, data, and processes to optimize customer satisfaction and loyalty.
Scope	Relationship Marketing is a broader marketing philosophy that encompasses all aspects of building and maintaining relationships with customers.	CRM is a specific approach, often supported by technology, processes, and strategies, for managing interactions with customers throughout the entire customer lifecycle.
Focus	Emphasizes the overall philosophy and strategies for building relationships with customers. It extends beyond technology and includes principles like customer-centricity, two-way communication, and mutual value creation.	Primarily focuses on the technology, processes, and tools used to manage and optimize customer interactions. It is more specific and operational in its approach, often involving the use of CRM software.
Implementation	Involves various strategies such as personalized communication, community building, and customer-centric policies. It may or may not rely heavily on technological tools.	Involves the use of CRM software and technology to capture, store, and analyze customer data. It also includes process automation, collaboration tools, and analytics to manage customer relationships efficiently.
Time Horizon	Focuses on building long-term relationships with customers, considering the entire customer lifecycle.	Manages customer interactions at various stages of the customer lifecycle, with an emphasis on optimizing each interaction for efficiency and effectiveness.
Philosophy vs. System	Relationship Marketing is more of a marketing philosophy or approach that guides the overall mindset of the organization toward customer relationships.	CRM is a system or strategy with a specific set of tools and processes designed to facilitate and enhance customer interactions.
Flexibility	Offers a more flexible and adaptable approach, allowing businesses to incorporate various relationship-building strategies based on their specific context and customer needs.	While flexible in its own right, CRM systems often have predefined structures and processes that may require some customization to fit specific business requirements

RELATIONSHIP DEVELOPMENT STRATEGIES

Relationship development strategies involve intentional efforts to build and strengthen connections with others, whether in personal or professional settings. The various relationship development strategies are explained as under:

Active Listening:

Paying full attention to what others are saying, showing genuine interest, and responding thoughtfully. For example, in a friendship, active listening involves fully engaging in a conversation, asking follow-up questions, and expressing empathy.

Effective Communication:

Clearly expressing thoughts and feelings while being mindful of the impact of words. For example, in a work setting, effective communication involves conveying ideas clearly in meetings and responding to emails promptly.

Building Trust:

Consistently demonstrating reliability, integrity, and transparency to earn and maintain trust. For example, a manager builds trust with their team by keeping promises, being honest about challenges, and delivering on commitments.

Shared Experiences:

Creating and participating in activities together to strengthen bonds and create shared memories. For example, friends attending a music concert together, enjoying the experience and deepening their connection through shared enjoyment.

Mutual Support:

Providing assistance, encouragement, and understanding to each other during both good and challenging times. For example, siblings supporting each other through academic challenges, celebrating successes, and offering comfort during setbacks.

Empathy:

Understanding and sharing the feelings of others, showing compassion and emotional support. For example, colleagues expressing empathy when a team member faces a personal difficulty, fostering a supportive work environment.

Networking:

Actively seeking and creating connections with professionals in the same or related fields. For example, attending industry conferences and engaging in networking events to build professional relationships and potential collaborations.

Mentorship:

Seeking guidance and advice from experienced individuals in a particular field to foster professional growth. For example, a new employee seeking mentorship from a seasoned colleague to gain insights and navigate their career path.

ORGANISATIONAL PERVASIVE APPROACH

An organizational pervasive approach refers to a strategy or mindset that permeates throughout an entire organization, influencing its culture, values, and operations. Certain examples of organizational pervasive approach are as under:

Customer-Centricity:

Placing customers at the center of all decisions and actions within the organization. For example, amazon's customer-centric approach is evident in its focus on delivering a seamless shopping experience, personalized recommendations, and efficient customer service.

Innovation Focus:

Prioritizing innovation and creativity as a core value throughout the organization. For example, Google's pervasive approach to innovation is seen in its encouragement of employees to spend a portion of their time on personal projects, leading to the development of new products and features.

Employee Empowerment:

Empowering employees at all levels to make decisions and contribute to the organization's success. For example, Zappos is known for its pervasive approach to employee empowerment, allowing customer service representatives to use their judgment to create exceptional customer experiences.

Integration into Operations - Sustainability:

Infusing sustainable practices into every aspect of the organization's operations. For example, Unilever's pervasive approach to sustainability involves sustainable sourcing, reducing environmental impact, and promoting social responsibility in its supply chain.

Quality Focus:

Prioritizing and maintaining high-quality standards in all products and services. For example, Toyota's pervasive approach to quality, known as the Toyota Production System, emphasizes continuous improvement and defect prevention in manufacturing.

Alignment with Organizational Goals:

Ensuring that the pervasive approach aligns with the organization's overall strategic goals. For example, a tech company adopting an innovation-focused pervasive approach aligns this strategy with the goal of staying ahead in a competitive market.

Adaptability:

Fostering a culture of adaptability and flexibility to respond to changing external factors. For example, IBM's pervasive approach to adaptability includes continuous learning and skill development to stay relevant in the rapidly evolving tech industry.

Customer Feedback Integration:

Actively incorporating customer feedback into decision-making processes. For example, Airbnb's pervasive approach involves using customer reviews and feedback to enhance the user experience and address areas for improvement.

MANAGING CUSTOMERS EMOTIONS

Managing customers' emotions is a crucial aspect of providing excellent customer service. Customer emotions play a significant role in their overall experience and satisfaction with a product or service. For example, a customer who feels heard and valued is more likely to become a loyal customer, while a negative emotional experience may lead to dissatisfaction and loss of business.

Techniques for Managing Customer Emotions:

Active Listening:

Paying full attention to customers, acknowledging their concerns, and responding appropriately. For example, a customer service representative listens patiently to a customer's complaint, repeats the issue to show understanding, and proposes a solution.

Empathy:

Putting yourself in the customer's shoes, understanding their feelings, and responding with genuine care. For example, a customer support agent expresses empathy by saying, "I understand how frustrating this situation must be for you. Let me see how I can help."

Positive Language and Tone:

Using positive and reassuring language, along with a friendly and helpful tone. For example, Instead of saying, "We can't do that," saying, "While that's a bit challenging, let me explore some alternative solutions for you."

Timely Responses:

Responding to customer inquiries and issues promptly to show that their concerns are a priority. For example, a company responds to customer emails or social media comments within a few hours, demonstrating a commitment to quick resolution.

Surprise and Delight:

Going above and beyond customer expectations to create positive emotions. For example, a hotel surprises a guest with a complimentary room upgrade on their birthday, creating a memorable and positive experience.

Dealing with Negative Emotions:

Apology and Ownership:

Taking responsibility for mistakes and offering a sincere apology. For example, a restaurant manager apologizes for a delayed order, takes ownership of the mistake, and provides a discount on the customer's next visit.

Resolution and Follow-Up:

Resolving customer issues promptly and following up to ensure satisfaction. For example, a tech support agent not only fixes a customer's technical issue but also follows up a day later to ensure the problem hasn't recurred.

Feedback Collection:

Actively seeking customer feedback to understand their emotions and experiences. For example, an e-commerce platform sends a post-purchase survey to gather feedback on the buying process and product satisfaction.

BRAND BUILDING THROUGH RELATIONSHIP MARKETING

Building a brand through relationship marketing involves creating strong and positive connections with customers over time. Relationship marketing is a strategy that focuses on building long-term relationships with customers by understanding and fulfilling their needs and preferences. For example, a local bakery sends personalized birthday discounts to its regular customers, creating a sense of connection and loyalty.

Importance of Relationships in Brand Building:

Strong relationships with customers lead to brand loyalty, positive word-of-mouth, and a positive brand image. For example, a clothing brand that engages with customers on social media, responds to comments, and shares user-generated content builds a community around its brand.

Strategies for Brand Building through Relationship Marketing:

Customer-Centric Approach:

Prioritize the needs and preferences of customers in all business decisions. For example, Starbucks creates a personalized experience by allowing customers to customize their drinks, fostering a sense of individuality.

Consistent Brand Messaging:

Ensure that your brand communicates a consistent message across all channels. For example: Nike's "Just Do It" slogan is consistently used in advertising, reinforcing the brand's message of empowerment.

Personalization:

Tailor products, services, and communications to individual customer preferences. For example, amazon suggests products based on past purchases, creating a personalized shopping experience for each customer.

Engagement and Communication:

Actively communicate with customers, respond to feedback, and engage in two-way communication. For example, Wendy's, a fast-food chain, is known for its humorous and engaging social media presence, interacting directly with customers.

Building Emotional Connections:

Share compelling stories about the brand's values, mission, and impact. For example, TOMS Shoes tells the story of its "One for One" model, where a pair of shoes is donated for every pair purchased, creating an emotional connection with customers who want to contribute to a social cause.

Surprise and Delight:

Exceed customer expectations by providing unexpected positive experiences. For example, Airbnb occasionally upgrades guests to premium accommodations for free, creating a delightful and memorable experience.

Loyalty Programs and Rewards:

Offer incentives and rewards for repeat business and brand loyalty. For example, Starbucks rewards allows customers to earn points for every purchase, leading to free drinks and exclusive discounts.

Further provide special offers and discounts to loyal customers. For example, Sephora's Beauty Insider program offers exclusive promotions and early access to sales for its loyal customers.

Events and Collaborations:

Host events or collaborate with influencers to bring customers together. For example, Apple's product launch events create a sense of excitement and community among Apple enthusiasts.

SERVICE LEVEL AGREEMENTS (April, 2023; Nov. 2022; Nov. 2019; Nov. 2018)

Service Level Agreements (SLAs) are agreements that define the level of service a customer can expect from a service provider. It is a formal agreement between a service provider and a customer that outlines the expected level of service, including performance metrics, responsibilities, and consequences for not meeting the agreed-upon standards. For example, imagine you hire a company to provide internet service. The SLA would specify the speed of the internet, uptime guarantees, and what happens if the service is not up to par.

Key Components of an SLA:

Service Metrics: Define specific measures of service performance, such as response time, resolution time, or system availability. Clearly, outline the responsibilities of both the service provider and the customer. Detail the consequences or penalties for not meeting the agreed-upon service levels. For example, specifies the maximum time it should take for the service provider to respond to a customer's inquiry or issue or an SLA might state that the service provider will respond to customer support tickets within 24 hours.

Resolution Time Metric:

Outlines the maximum time allowed to resolve a customer's issue or provide a solution. For example, the SLA could state that critical issues must be resolved within 4 hours, while non-critical issues have a resolution time of 24 hours.

Uptime Guarantee:

Ensures a minimum level of system availability or uptime. For example, an SLA for a cloud service might guarantee 99.9% uptime, meaning the service should be available 99.9% of the time in a given period.

Consequences and Penalties:

Describes the consequences or penalties if the service provider fails to meet the agreed-upon service levels. For example, the SLA might state that if the service provider does not meet the uptime guarantee, customers will receive a credit on their next invoice.

Compensation:

Explanation: Outlines any compensation or remedies offered to the customer in case of service level breaches.

Example: If the service provider fails to meet the agreed-upon response times consistently, they might offer customers a discount on their subscription fees.

Regular Review and Adjustment:

Specifies how often the SLA will be reviewed, and if necessary, updated based on changing circumstances. For example, the SLA might state that a review will be conducted annually, with adjustments made as needed to reflect changes in technology or customer needs.

Communication Protocols:

Defines the communication channels and protocols for reporting issues, changes, or updates related to the SLA. For example, the SLA could outline that customers should submit support requests through a designated ticketing system for tracking and resolution.

RELATIONSHIP CHALLENGES

Communication Gaps:

Inadequate communication between the company and customers can lead to misunderstandings and dissatisfaction. For example, a customer may feel frustrated if they are not informed about changes in product features or service policies.

Data Inconsistency:

Inaccurate or inconsistent customer data can hinder effective communication and personalization. For example, sending promotional emails with incorrect customer names or outdated information can create a negative impression.

Lack of Personalization:

Failing to tailor interactions based on individual customer preferences and history. For example, a company sending generic marketing messages without considering the specific interests of its diverse customer base.

Unresolved Customer Issues:

Inability to address and resolve customer problems promptly can lead to dissatisfaction. For example, if a customer reports a product defect and the company doesn't address it in a timely manner, the customer may lose trust.

Overreliance on Technology:

Depending too heavily on CRM systems without human touch can make interactions feel impersonal. For example, automated responses to customer queries without human intervention may lead to frustration if the issue is complex.

QUESTIONS

Multiple choice questions (MCQs):

a. An_____ customer is from outside the organization providing the product or service,
   (i)External (ii) Internal (iii) Active (iv) Passive
b. _____ type of customers stands out as being the most trend-oriented and product-focused.
   (i)Content Streamer (ii) Savvy Maximiser (iii) Undaunted Striver (iv) Secure Traditionalist
c. _____ type of customer is driven by value. He makes impulsive decisions.
   (i)Content Streamer (ii) Savvy Maximiser (iii) Undaunted Striver (iv)Secure Traditionalist
d. _____ type of customer is suspicious of everyone, believing that all people are selfish.

Customer Relationship Management

(i) Content Streamer (ii) Savvy Maximiser (iii) Undaunted Striver (iv) Secure Traditionalist

e. _____ type of customer knows just what they want and do not want to try any other goods or services.
(i) Content Streamer (ii) Savvy Maximiser (iii) Undaunted Striver (iv) Secure Traditionalist

f. _____ is a component of CRM. (Oct.18)
(i) People (ii) Technology (iii) Information (iv) All of the above

g. CRM is a discipline that covers all _____ needed to build successful relationship with customers. (May19)
(i) Essential (ii) Elements (iii) Equipment's (iv) Endeavors

h. CRM saves expensive data _____ time. (May19)
(i) Membership (ii) Management (iii) Movements (iv) None of these

i. The _____ tier describe the company's most profitable customers. (May19)
(i) Gold (ii) Platinum (iii) Iron (iv) Lead

j. _____ refers to any marketing activity that interrupts" a viewer's attention.
(i) Interruption Marketing (ii) Permission Marketing (iii) Transactional Marketing (iv) Relationship Marketing

k. _____ is the way to make advertising work effectively.
(i) Interruption Marketing (ii) Permission Marketing (iii) Transactional Marketing (iv) Relationship Marketing

l. _____ is a business strategy that focuses on "single point of sale" transaction.
(i) Interruption Marketing (ii) Permission Marketing (iii) Transactional Marketing (iv) Relationship Marketing

m. _____ is a business strategy that seeks to establish long term relationship with its customer rather than focusing on a single transaction.
(i) Interruption Marketing (ii) Permission Marketing (iii) Transactional Marketing (iv) Relationship Marketing

n. _____ is a set of methods, strategies, and applications that facilitate a company to manage customer relationships.
(i) Customer Relationship (ii) Customer Relationship Management (iii) Customer Lifetime Value (iv) Relationship Marketing

o. _____ are repeated interactive discussions among randomly selected customers.
(i) Group discussion (ii) Focus group interviews (iii) Debates (iv) Relationship Marketing

p. CRM and relationship marketing focus on customer retention and _____. (May19)
(i) Mutuality (ii) Loyalty (iii) Treaty (iv) Popularity

q. A service level agreement (SLA) is a tool for building _____ relationship with high value customers. (Nov19)
(i) Formal (ii) Informal (iii) Shared (iv) None

Answer:- (a-i), (b-iii), (c-ii), (d-i), (e-iv), (f-iv), (g-ii), (h-ii), (i-ii), (j-i), (k-ii), (l-iii), (m-iv), (n-ii), (o-ii), (p-ii), (q-i)

Fill in the blanks:

a. Someone who buys goods and services _____.

Customer Relationship Management

b. _____ customers stand out as being the most trend-oriented and product-focused.
c. _____ customers make impulsive decisions.
d. _____ types of customers know just what they want and do not want to try any other goods or services.
e. A database that collects information about all the customers is known as_____.
f. CRM works on increasing customer_____.
g. CRM is a _____ business strategy that aims to increase customer satisfaction and customer loyalty by offering more responsive and customized services to each customer.
h. _____ is an intelligent strategy for selling goods or services to your customers that uses direct marketing tactics to ensure the customers stick with the membership for months or years.
i. _____ refers to any marketing activity that interrupts" a viewer's attention.
j. _____ is a business strategy that seeks to establish long-term relationship with its customers rather than focusing on a single transaction.
k. Transactional marketing is a business strategy that focuses on _____ point of sale transactions.
l. _____ is based on the quality of customer relationship, as experienced from that of customer and the marketer.
m. _____ is the result of cumulative net returns received over the lifetime of customers.
n. Calls from customers regarding their queries, problems, suggestions are handled by _____.

Answer:- (a) Customers (b) Undaunted Striver (c) Savvy Maximizer (d) Secured traditionalist (e) CRM (f) Loyalty (g) Customer-focused (h) Continuity Marketing (i) Interruption Marketing (j) Relationship Marketing (k) Single (l) Customer value (m) Customer Lifetime Value (CLV) (n) Call Centres

True or False:-

a. Analytical CRM provides support to "front office" business process.
b. Operational CRM analyses customer data for a variety purpose. It applies to the marketing level and aims to propose an indebt marketing analysis.
c. Sales Intelligence CRM is similar to analytical CRM but is intended as a more direct sales tool.
d. CRM management combines elements of operational and analytical CRM.
e. Collaborative CRM covers aspects of a company's dealings with customers that are handled by various departments with a company, such as sales, technical support, and marketing.
f. CRM is used as synonyms to Relationship marketing, which took place back into the pre-industrial era in the form of interaction between producers of agricultural products and consumers.
g. Customers evolve from strangers to partners. (May 19)
h. CRM wastes the time and money of the service organization. (May 19)
i. Relationship Marketing refers to any marketing activity that "interrupts" a viewer's attention.
j. Interruption marketing is a way to make advertising work effectively.

k. Transactional marketing is a business strategy that focuses on a single point of sale transaction.
l. Customer relationship represents how much a customer is worth in terms of monetary value and therefore how much money should be spent on the acquisition and retention of that customer by the marketing department of the company.
m. Customer lifetime value is a set of methods, strategies and applications that facilitate a company to manage customer relationship.
n. A customer relationship agreement is a contract between a service provider and the end user that defines the level of service expected from service provider. (Oct18)
o. CRM maintains a relationship with customers by frequent contracts to obtain their maximum data.

Answer:- (a) False (b) False (c) True (d) False (e) True (f) True (g) True (h) False (i) False (j) False (k) True (l) False (m) False (n) True (o) False

Match the following: -

Sr. No.	Group 'A'	Sr. No.	Group 'B'
(a)	Initiator	(i)	Decision to Buy
(b)	Influencer	(ii)	Choose which product to buy
(c)	Decision Maker	(iii)	The person outside the group who influence
(d)	Buyer	(iv)	Suggest buying
(e)	Convenience	(v)	Product
(f)	Customer Value and benefits	(vi)	Place
(g)	Customer Lifetime Value	(vii)	Long-term Relationship
(h)	Relationship Marketing	(viii)	Advertising Work Effectively
(i)	Transactional Marketing	(ix)	Marketing activity that interrupts" a viewer attention
(j)	Interruption Marketing	(x)	Single point of sale transaction
(k)	Permission Marketing	(xi)	Monetary value

Answer:- (a-iv), (b-iii), (c-ii), (d-i), (e-vi), (f-v), (g-xi), (h-vii), (i-x), (j-ix), (k-viii)

Long-answer typed questions:

Q. Define CRM. Explain the components and evolution of customer relationships. (April, 2023; Nov. 2019; April, 2019)

Q. "An organization can perform brand building using relationship marketing"- Comment. (April, 2023; Nov. 2018)

Q. Explain the challenges and barriers in implementing CRM. (April, 2023; Nov. 2019; Nov. 2018)

Q. Write a short note on service-level agreement. (April, 2023; Nov. 2022; Nov. 2019; Nov. 2018)

Q. Explain the benefits of CRM to the customers as well as organizations. (Nov. 2022)

Q. Define CRM. Explain its objectives. (Nov. 2022; April, 2019).

Q. Define CRM. Explain its types. (Nov. 2022)

Q. Explain customer profitability segments. (April, 2019; Nov. 2018)

Customer Relationship Management

UNIT 2

CRM MARKETING INITIATIVES, CUSTOMER SERVICE AND DATA MANAGEMENT

- ✓ CRM marketing initiatives: cross selling and upselling
- ✓ Difference between cross-selling and up-selling

- ✓ Customer retention
- ✓ Customer retention strategy: customer complaint management, service recovery strategy, managing customer waiting strategy
- ✓ Ways to handle waiting time
- ✓ Levels of retention strategy:
- ✓ Brand switching
- ✓ Customer handling
- ✓ Behavior prediction
- ✓ Customer profitability and value modelling
- ✓ Channel optimization
- ✓ Personalization
- ✓ Event-based marketing
- ✓ CRM and customer service
- ✓ Techniques of improving customer service
    1. Customer care software
    2. Multimedia contact center deliveries
    3. Call center and customer care
    4. Call routing
    5. Contact center sales support
    6. Web-based self service
    7. Customer satisfaction measurement
    8. Call scripting
    9. Cyber agents
    10. Workforce management
- ✓ CRM and data management
- ✓ Types of data
- ✓ Identifying data quality issues
- ✓ Planning and getting information quality
- ✓ Using tools to manage the data
- ✓ Data analysis
- ✓ Data mining
- ✓ Online analytical processing (OLAP)
- ✓ Clickstream analysis
- ✓ Personalization:
- ✓ Collaborative filtering
- ✓ Data reporting
- ✓ Questions

CRM MARKETING INITIATIVES: CROSS SELLING AND UPSELLING (April, 2019)

Cross-selling:

Cross-selling is the strategy of offering customers complementary products or services that are related to their initial purchase. CRM systems track customer preferences and purchase history. For instance, if a CRM system identifies a customer who frequently buys cameras, it can prompt the sales team to suggest related items like camera bags or lenses. Cross-selling enhances customer satisfaction by providing them with additional products they might find useful. It can also increase revenue for the business. For example, A customer went to

McDonalds to buy a burger, After, placing an order for burger, the cashier will suggest you to add French fries or milkshake or both to the previous order because of attractive benefits in terms of discounts.

Few more examples of cross-selling are:

- A customer buys a smartphone, a cross-selling approach would be to suggest accessories like a phone case, screen protector, or headphones.
- A life insurance company suggesting its customer sign up for car or health insurance.
- A wholesale mobile retailer suggesting a customer choose a network or carrier after buying a mobile.
- A laptop seller offering a customer a mouse, pen-drive, and/or accessories.
- A hospitality brand offering tours and experiences to guests after booking the accommodation.

Benefits of Cross-selling

Benefits of Cross-selling to the Buyer:

1. One stop shopping
2. More customized service.
3. Savings in transaction costs
4. Synegy effect

Benefits of Cross-selling to the Seller:

1. Increasing revenue per customer
2. Reducing competition.
3. Savings in transaction costs
4. Synergy effects
5. Decreasing acquisition expenses
6. Economies of scope

Pitfalls of Cross-selling

1. *Ineffective Product Pairing*:
   Recommending products that don't complement the customer's original purchase can lead to dissatisfaction. For example, if a customer buys a laptop, suggesting unrelated items like kitchen appliances might not resonate well and may result in the customer feeling that the recommendations are irrelevant.
2. *Pushy Sales Tactics*:
   Being too aggressive in pushing additional products can make customers uncomfortable and may negatively impact the overall shopping experience. For example, a customer purchasing a smartphone may feel overwhelmed if the salesperson insists on buying various accessories, creating a pushy atmosphere.
3. *Ignoring Customer Needs*:
   Not paying attention to the customer's actual needs and preferences can result in recommendations that don't align with what the customer values. For example, suggesting a high-end camera to a customer who primarily takes casual photos with a smartphone may not meet their actual needs and could lead to dissatisfaction.
4. *Limited Communication*:

Failing to communicate the value or benefits of the additional products may result in customers being unaware of why they should consider the cross-sell. For example, if a customer is offered extended warranty options without understanding the benefits, they may decline the offer due to a lack of perceived value.

Upselling:

Upselling involves encouraging customers to buy a higher-end product or add premium features to their purchase, thereby increasing the overall sale value. CRM tools analyze customer behavior and spending patterns. If a customer often buys mid-range smartphones, the system might prompt the sales team to recommend a premium model that aligns with the customer's preferences. Upselling boosts revenue by encouraging customers to spend more on higher-value products or premium features. It can also contribute to customer loyalty if the upsell adds significant value. For example, A customer went to McDonalds to buy a small burger, After, placing an order for small burger, the casher asked to buy the large burger instead of small one as cost of large burger is only 1.5 times of small burger.

Few more examples of up-selling are:

- if a customer is looking at a basic laptop, an upselling tactic would be to highlight a more advanced model with better specifications and features, such as increased storage or faster processing speed.
- Selling an extended service contract for an appliance.
- Suggesting that a customer opt on a vehicle, such as leather upholstery.
- Suggesting that a customer purchase a more extensive car wash package.
- A television brand suggesting its customer to go for home-theatre of its brand.

Benefits of up-selling:

1. Increases order value
2. Increases customer satisfaction
3. Benefit of referrals
4. Increases loyalty
5. Increases life-time

DIFFERENCE BETWEEN CROSS-SELLING AND UP-SELLING

Basis	Cross-selling	Up-selling
Definition	This involves offering customers additional products or services that are related or complementary to their initial purchase.	This strategy involves encouraging customers to buy a more expensive or premium version of the product they are considering or adding features to increase the overall sale value.
Focus on the Purchase	The emphasis is on expanding the customer's purchase by suggesting	The emphasis is on convincing the customer to spend more by

Basis	Cross-selling	Up-selling
	related items that enhance or complement the main product.	choosing a higher-end product or adding premium features.
Customer Benefit	Enhances the customer's experience by providing them with additional items that add value to their initial purchase.	Offers the customer an opportunity to enjoy higher-end features, improved performance, or greater capabilities by opting for a more premium product.
Goal	The primary goal is to increase the breadth of the customer's purchase, introducing them to a variety of products.	The primary goal is to increase the depth of the customer's purchase, encouraging them to spend more on a single, higher-value item.
Implementation	Often occurs during the checkout process or through targeted recommendations based on the customer's purchase history.	Can be implemented by highlighting premium options, offering upgrade suggestions, or providing bundle deals that encourage customers to choose a more expensive product.
Example	While buying laptop, seller suggests to buy printer along with it.	While buying laptop of 13-inch screen, the seller suggests to buy a laptop of 15-inch screen.

CUSTOMER RETENTION (Nov. 2022; Nov. 2019)

Customer retention means keeping existing customers happy and engaged to ensure they continue buying from a business over time. It's like having friends who enjoy spending time with you regularly. For businesses, keeping customers is important because it's easier and more profitable than constantly finding new ones. For example, you have a favorite toy store. They always have the toys you love, the staff is nice, and sometimes they give you special discounts. You keep going back because it feels like your special place. For businesses, customer retention is about creating that special feeling so people keep coming back for more fun!

Ways to Retain the Customers:

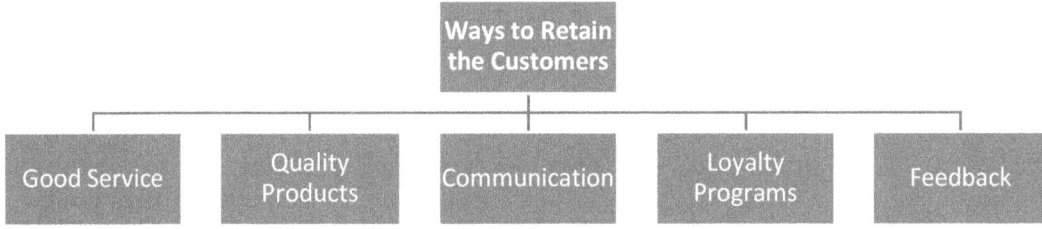

1. *Good Service*:
   Treat customers nicely and make sure they have a good experience. For example, a friendly waiter who remembers your favorite dish at a restaurant.
2. *Quality Products*:
   Offer products that customers love and find valuable. For example, a phone company making durable and reliable smartphones.
3. *Communication*:
   Stay in touch with customers to know what they need and want. For example, sending emails about new products or special deals.
4. *Loyalty Programs*:
   Reward customers for choosing your business regularly. For example, a coffee shop offering a free drink after a certain number of purchases.
5. *Feedback*:
   Ask customers for their thoughts to improve your services. For example, a survey after a hotel stay to understand what guests liked or disliked.

CUSTOMER RETENTION STRATEGY

Customer Retention Strategy

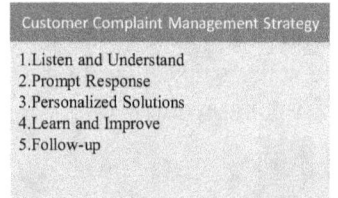
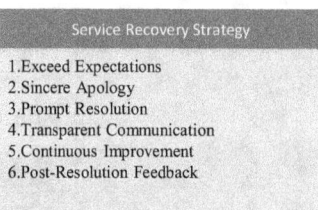
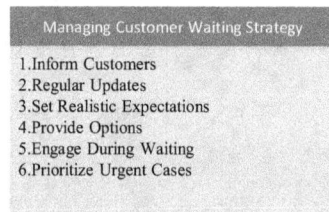

There are mainly three customer retention strategies:

1. Customer Complaint Management Strategy
2. Service Recovery Strategy
3. Managing Customer Waiting Strategy

Customer Complaint Management:

Customer complaint management refers to the process of effectively handling and addressing customer complaints or concerns in a business or organizational setting. It involves a systematic approach to receiving, documenting, evaluating, and resolving customer complaints to ensure customer satisfaction and maintain a positive relationship with the customer.

Customer Complaint Management Strategies:

1. *Listen and Understand*
   Train your team to listen carefully to customer complaints. Understand the issue before responding. For instance, if a customer is upset about a late delivery, make sure you comprehend the specific problem.
2. *Prompt Response*
   Respond swiftly to customer complaints. Acknowledge the problem, and let them know you're actively working on a solution. If a customer emails about a defective product, reply promptly, express understanding, and outline the steps for a return or replacement.
3. *Personalized Solutions*

Provide personalized solutions. If a customer receives a damaged item, don't just replace it. Offer a discount on their next purchase or an extra item as a goodwill gesture. This shows them that you value their satisfaction and are willing to go the extra mile.

4. *Learn and Improve*

   Use complaints as learning opportunities. If customers consistently complain about a particular issue, analyze it, and implement improvements. For instance, if many customers express frustration about a confusing checkout process on your website, work on simplifying it.

5. *Follow-up*

   After resolving a complaint, follow up with the customer. Ask if the solution met their expectations and if there's anything else you can do. If a customer complained about a delayed service, check in afterward to ensure they are now satisfied with the timeliness.

Service Recovery Strategy:

Service recovery refers to the actions taken by a business or service provider to address and resolve a customer's concerns or complaints after a service failure or a negative experience. The goal of service recovery is to retain the customer's loyalty, restore their confidence in the business, and potentially turn a negative experience into a positive one.

Service Recovery Strategies:

1. *Exceed Expectations*

   When things go wrong, aim to exceed customer expectations in fixing the issue. If a customer receives a damaged product, not only replace it but also offer a discount on their next purchase. This demonstrates your commitment to making things right and adds a positive touch to the resolution.

2. *Sincere Apology*

   Begin the service recovery process with a sincere apology. If a customer experiences a delay in service, acknowledge their inconvenience, apologize for it, and assure them that you're actively working on a solution. This empathetic approach helps rebuild trust.

3. *Prompt Resolution*

   Act quickly to resolve issues. If a customer faces a billing error, address it promptly and ensure they receive a corrected invoice. This swift action not only resolves the problem but also demonstrates your commitment to customer satisfaction.

4. *Transparent Communication*

   Be transparent about the steps you're taking to rectify the situation. If there's a delay in delivering a service, communicate the reasons behind it and provide realistic timelines for resolution. Open communication helps manage customer expectations.

5. *Continuous Improvement*

   Treat service issues as opportunities to learn and improve. If multiple customers report the same problem, analyze it, and implement changes to prevent its recurrence. For instance, if customers consistently complain about a certain feature in your app, consider updating it based on their feedback.

6. *Post-Resolution Feedback*

   After resolving a service issue, follow up with the customer. Ask if the solution met their expectations and if there's anything else you can do to enhance their experience. This post-resolution engagement reinforces your commitment to customer satisfaction.

Managing Customer Waiting Strategy:

Managing customer waiting refers to the process of handling and optimizing the time customers spend waiting for a service or product. Waiting times can occur in various contexts, such as retail stores, restaurants, call centers, or other service-oriented businesses. Effectively managing customer waiting is crucial for providing a positive customer experience.

Managing Customer Waiting Strategies

1. *Inform Customers*
   If there's a delay in providing a service or product, communicate the reasons clearly. For instance, if an online order will take longer to ship due to unexpected demand, inform customers promptly. Transparent communication helps manage expectations and reduces frustration.
2. *Regular Updates*
   Keep customers in the loop during waiting periods. If there's a delay in processing their request, send periodic updates. This could be a simple email or notification, assuring them that their order is being worked on and providing an estimated completion time.
3. *Set Realistic Expectations*
   When communicating timelines, set realistic expectations. If you anticipate a service will take a week, tell customers it might take ten days. If you then deliver in seven days, it exceeds their expectations and leaves them pleasantly surprised.
4. *Provide Options*
   If a customer faces a waiting period, offer alternatives to meet their needs in the meantime. For instance, if a particular product is out of stock, suggest a similar item or provide a discount for their patience. This shows a commitment to customer satisfaction even in the face of delays.
5. *Engage During Waiting*
   If applicable, create an engaging waiting experience. For instance, if customers are on hold during a customer service call, play informative messages or offer promotions. This keeps them engaged and makes the wait seem less tedious.
6. *Prioritize Urgent Cases*
   If there are varying degrees of urgency, prioritize cases accordingly. For example, if a customer has an urgent issue, ensure their request is handled faster than routine ones. This demonstrates responsiveness and a customer-centric approach.

WAYS TO HANDLE WAITING TIME

1. **Unoccupied Time Feels Longer Than Occupied Time**:
   When you're not doing anything, time feels like it's dragging. That's why places like waiting rooms have magazines, TVs, or even snacks to keep you busy. It makes waiting feel shorter.
2. **Pre and Post Process Waits Feel Longer Than In-Process Waits**:
   Waiting before or after the main event feels longer. Waiting to enter a theme park or for the bill at a restaurant seems longer than waiting for a ride or during your meal.
3. **Anxiety Makes Waits Seem Longer**:
   If you're anxious while waiting, time feels slower. For example, waiting for someone and worrying about the meeting time or place can make the wait feel much longer.
4. **Uncertain Waits Are Longer Than Known Finite Waits**:
   Waiting is easier when you know how long it will take. Waiting for a delayed flight without knowing when it will leave is more stressful because the end is uncertain.
5. **Unexplained Waits Are Longer Than Explained Waits**:
   Waiting without knowing why is hard. Imagine being in an elevator that stops unexpectedly. Not knowing what's happening or how long you'll be stuck makes the wait feel longer.
6. **Unfair Waits Are Longer Than Equitable Waits**:

People get upset if they think others are getting special treatment. In some places, it's expected to wait your turn. Jumping ahead can make the wait seem unfair.

7. **The More Valuable the Service, the Longer People Will Wait**:
People are willing to wait longer for something important or valuable. For instance, waiting in line for hours to get good seats at a popular concert or sports event.

8. **Uncomfortable Waits Feel Longer Than Comfortable Waits**:
Waiting is harder if you're uncomfortable. Standing in line becomes more burdensome if it's too hot, too cold, or if there's no protection from the weather.

9. **Unfamiliar Waits Seem Longer Than Familiar Ones**:
Knowing what to expect makes waiting easier. Regular users of a service are more comfortable waiting because they are familiar with the process, while new users may feel more anxious.

Levels of Retention Strategy:

There are four levels of retention strategies:

1. Financial Bonds
2. Social Bonds
3. Customization Bonds
4. Structural Bonds

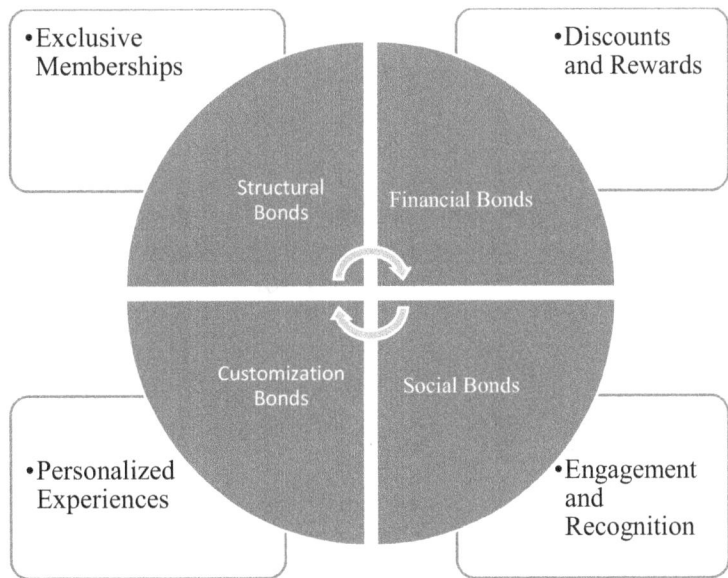

Financial Bonds (Basic Retention):

Offer financial incentives to customers who make repeat purchases. For instance, provide a discount on their next purchase or introduce a loyalty program where they earn points for every transaction, which can be redeemed for discounts or free items.

Social Bonds (Intermediate Retention):

Build social bonds by engaging with customers on social media platforms. Respond to comments, share user-generated content, and publicly acknowledge loyal customers. This creates a sense of community and connection.

Customization Bonds (Advanced Retention):

Create customization bonds by tailoring your products or services to individual customer preferences. If you have an online store, use personalized recommendations based on their previous purchases or browsing history. This makes customers feel valued and understood.

Structural Bonds (Expert Retention):

Establish structural bonds by creating exclusive memberships or VIP programs. Provide members with access to special events, early product releases, or premium customer support. This structural bond encourages long-term commitment.

BRAND SWITCHING

Brand switching refers to the consumer behavior of moving from one brand to another within a particular product or service category. This can occur for various reasons, and understanding these motivations is crucial for businesses to retain customers and attract new ones. Here are some common reasons for brand switching:

Price:

Consumers often switch brands in search of better prices or discounts. If a competitor offers a similar product or service at a lower cost, customers may be inclined to switch.

Quality:

Perceived or actual differences in quality can drive brand switching. If a consumer believes that a competing brand offers a superior product, they may switch to that brand for a better experience.

Innovation:

Some consumers are attracted to brands that consistently introduce new and innovative products or services. If a brand fails to keep up with market trends or technological advancements, customers may switch to a more forward-thinking competitor.

Customer Service:

Poor customer service experiences can drive customers away. A company that provides excellent customer service is more likely to retain its customer base, while those with subpar service may lose customers to competitors.

Brand Image and Values:

Consumers may switch brands if they feel a stronger alignment with the values and image of a competitor. Brands that resonate with their target audience on a personal or social level are more likely to retain customer loyalty.

Availability and Accessibility:

If a preferred brand is not readily available or accessible, consumers may switch to a more convenient option. This is particularly relevant in industries where convenience and accessibility are critical factors.

Promotions and Marketing:

Effective marketing strategies, promotions, and advertising can influence consumer choices. If a competitor runs compelling campaigns, consumers may be enticed to switch brands.

Customer Relationship Management

Personal Recommendations:

Word-of-mouth and personal recommendations play a significant role in brand switching. If friends, family, or influencers endorse a different brand, consumers may be motivated to try it.

Negative Experiences:

Negative experiences with a particular brand, such as product defects, recalls, or ethical concerns, can prompt consumers to switch to a more reliable or morally aligned alternative.

CUSTOMER HANDLING

Customer handling refers to the process of managing interactions and relationships with customers. It involves addressing customer inquiries, concerns, and feedback to ensure their satisfaction. Effective customer handling is crucial for building and maintaining positive relationships with customers, which, in turn, contributes to customer loyalty and business success.

Customer Handling Strategy:

1. *Friendly and Empathetic Communication*
   Train your team to respond to customers in a friendly and empathetic manner. For instance, if a customer is upset about a delayed delivery, respond with understanding and a sincere apology, acknowledging their frustration. Further Respond promptly to customer inquiries. Whether it's a question about a product or a concern, a quick response demonstrates attentiveness and a commitment to addressing their needs promptly.
2. *Personalization in Interactions*
   Tailor your interactions based on customer preferences. If a customer frequently buys a particular product, recommend similar items they might like. Personalization shows that you value their individual needs.
3. *Problem Resolution Skills*

Equip your team with problem-solving skills. If a customer encounters an issue, ensure your representatives can efficiently identify and implement solutions. This might involve offering refunds, replacements, or other forms of compensation.
4. *Proactive Communication*
Be proactive in addressing potential concerns. If a product is out of stock, inform customers in advance and suggest alternatives. Proactive communication shows foresight and a dedication to customer satisfaction.
5. *Follow-up and Feedback Requests*
After a customer makes a purchase, follow up with a thank-you message and ask for feedback. This not only shows appreciation but also provides valuable insights into their experience, helping you continually improve.
6. *Loyalty Programs and Rewards*
Implement a loyalty program that rewards repeat customers. For example, offer exclusive discounts or early access to new products. This encourages customers to stay engaged with your brand.

BEHAVIOR PREDICTION (April, 2023)

Behavior Prediction refers to the anticipation of customer actions and preferences based on their past interactions with a business. Understanding and predicting customer behavior is crucial for businesses to provide personalized and tailored experiences, fostering long-term relationships.

Importance of Behavior Prediction:

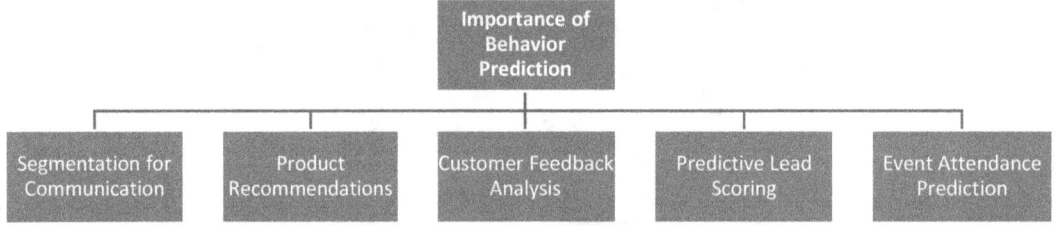

1. *Segmentation for Communication*:
CRM systems can predict which communication channels a customer prefers based on past interactions. For example, if a customer frequently engages with email updates but rarely clicks on SMS messages, the CRM might predict a preference for email communication.
2. *Product Recommendations*:
CRM tools predict the products or services a customer is likely to be interested in based on their previous purchases. For example, if a customer frequently buys athletic shoes, the CRM might suggest new releases or related sports gear.
3. *Customer Feedback Analysis*:
CRM systems analyze past feedback to predict areas of improvement or features that customers are likely to appreciate. For example, if a customer consistently provides feedback about faster shipping, the CRM may predict a preference for expedited delivery options.
4. *Predictive Lead Scoring*:

CRM employs predictive analytics to score leads, indicating which potential customers are more likely to convert based on historical data. For example, if customers from a certain industry tend to convert more often, the CRM may prioritize leads from that industry.

5. *Event Attendance Prediction*:
CRM can predict whether a customer is likely to attend an event or webinar based on their history of participation. For example, if a customer regularly attends webinars on marketing strategies, the CRM might predict their interest in an upcoming marketing workshop.

CUSTOMER PROFITABILITY AND VALUE MODELLING (Nov. 2019; Nov. 2018)

Customer profitability and value modeling are important aspects of business strategy and management. Customer profitability is about understanding how much profit a business earns from each customer. It involves analyzing the revenue generated by a customer against the costs associated with acquiring, serving, and retaining that customer. For example, suppose a small bakery has two customers, Alice and Bob. Alice buys cakes worth ₹5,000 every week, and the cost to serve her is ₹3,000. Bob, on the other hand, buys pastries worth ₹2,000 every week, and the cost to serve him is ₹1,500. The bakery's profit from Alice is ₹2,000 (₹5,000 - ₹3,000), and from Bob, it's ₹500 (₹2,000- ₹1,500). This helps the bakery identify which customers contribute more to its profits. On the other side, value modeling involves assessing the value a customer brings to a business beyond just monetary transactions. It considers factors like brand loyalty, referrals, and long-term potential. For example, continuing with the bakery example, let's say Alice not only buys cakes regularly but also recommends the bakery to her friends. Bob, on the other hand, buys pastries but doesn't bring in any referrals. The value of Alice goes beyond the immediate profit - it includes the potential for more customers through her recommendations.

Key Steps in Customer Profitability and Value Modeling:

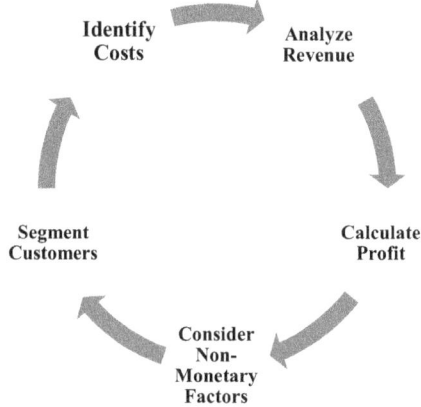

1. *Identify Costs*:
Break down costs associated with acquiring, serving, and retaining customers. This includes marketing costs, customer service expenses, and any loyalty programs.
2. *Analyze Revenue*:
Understand the revenue generated from each customer. This includes both the initial purchase and any subsequent transactions.
3. *Calculate Profit*:
Subtract the costs from the revenue to determine the profit generated by each customer.

4. *Consider Non-Monetary Factors*:
   Look at factors like customer loyalty, word-of-mouth referrals, and potential for long-term relationships to understand the broader value a customer brings.
5. *Segment Customers*:
6. Categorize customers based on their profitability and value. This segmentation can guide marketing and service strategies.

CHANNEL OPTIMIZATION

Channel optimization refers to the process of maximizing the efficiency and effectiveness of the various channels a business uses to reach and interact with its customers. In simple words, channels are the different avenues through which a business connects with its customers. This can be a website, a physical store, social media platforms, email, or any other means of communication. Channel optimization ensures that resources (time, money, effort) invested in each channel are used effectively. It maximizes the impact of each channel in reaching and engaging the target audience.

Steps in Channel Optimization:

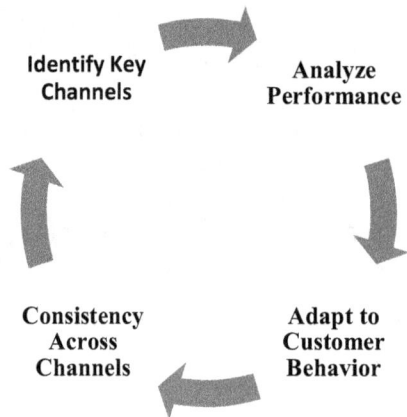

1. *Identify Key Channels*:
   Determine which channels are most relevant to your target audience. For example, if your customers are active on social media, optimizing those channels would be crucial.
2. *Analyze Performance*:
   Evaluate how each channel is performing. Look at metrics like customer engagement, conversion rates, and return on investment.
3. *Adapt to Customer Behavior*:
   Understand how your customers prefer to interact with your business. If they prefer online shopping, focus on optimizing your e-commerce platform. For example, an online clothing store optimizes its website for mobile users, recognizing that many customers shop from their smartphones.
4. *Consistency Across Channels*:
   Maintain a consistent brand image and messaging across all channels. This helps in building a coherent and recognizable brand.

PERSONALIZATION

Personalization in business refers to tailoring products, services, or experiences to meet the specific needs and preferences of individual customers. It's about making each customer feel unique and enhancing their interaction with a brand. In other words, personalization involves customizing various aspects of the customer experience based on individual characteristics such as preferences, behaviors, and demographics.

Types of Personalization:

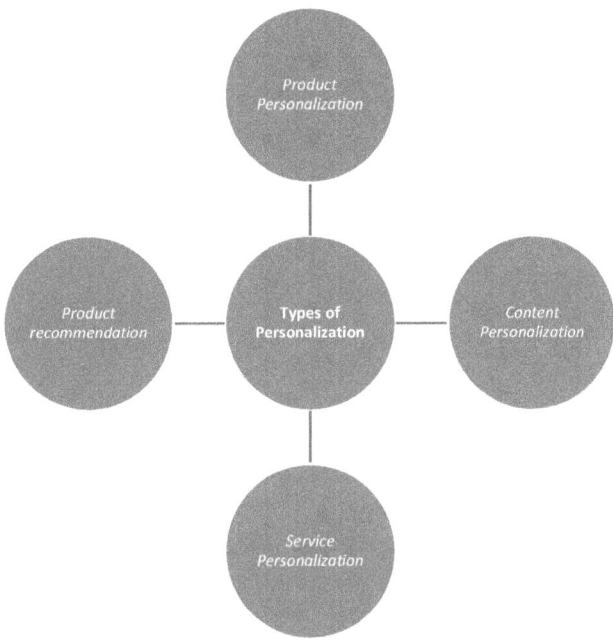

1. *Product Personalization*:
   Creating products with options for customization. For example, a shoe company allowing customers to choose colors and add personalized initials to their shoes.
2. *Content Personalization*:
   Tailoring content, such as emails or website recommendations, to match the interests and preferences of each customer. For instance, an online bookstore suggesting books based on a customer's past purchases.
3. *Service Personalization*:
   Providing personalized customer service experiences. For example, a hotel offering room preferences based on a guest's previous stays.
4. *Product recommendation*:
   Business recommends the products to the consumers on the basis of their previous history. For example, Amazon analyzes a customer's browsing and purchase history to provide personalized product recommendations. For instance, if a customer frequently buys science fiction books, Amazon may suggest new science fiction releases. Netflix uses algorithms to analyze a user's viewing history and preferences to recommend movies and TV shows that align with their taste. Starbucks' mobile app provides personalized offers and rewards based on a customer's previous purchases. For example, a customer who regularly buys lattes might receive a personalized discount on their favorite drink.

Benefits of Personalization:

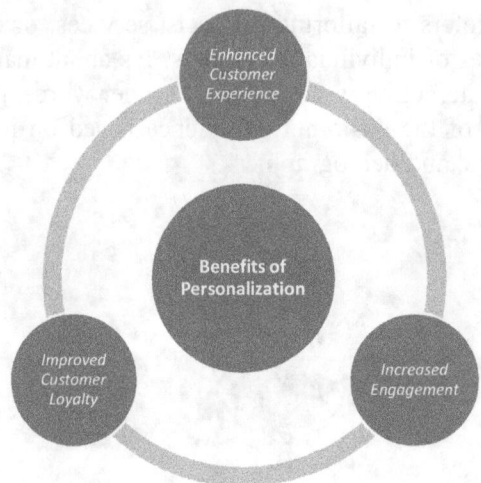

1. *Enhanced Customer Experience*:
   Customers feel more valued when products and services are tailored to their preferences, leading to a positive overall experience.
2. *Increased Engagement*:
   Personalized content or recommendations capture the attention of customers, increasing engagement with a brand.
3. *Improved Customer Loyalty*:
   When customers feel that a brand understands and caters to their individual needs, they are more likely to become loyal and repeat customers.

Steps in Implementation of Personalization:

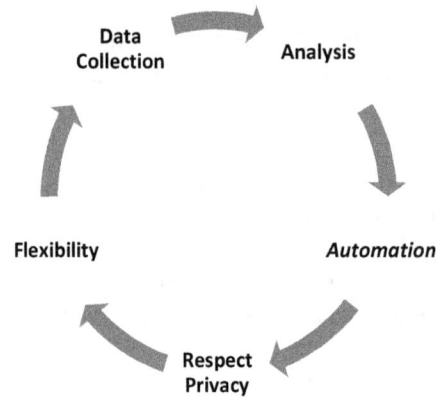

1. *Data Collection*:
   Collect relevant data about customers, such as purchase history, preferences, and feedback.
2. *Analysis*:
   Use data analytics tools to analyze customer information and identify patterns.
3. *Automation*:
   Implement automated systems to deliver personalized content, recommendations, or offers to customers.
4. *Respect Privacy*:
   Always prioritize customer privacy and obtain consent before collecting and using personal data.

Customer Relationship Management

5. *Flexibility*:
   Recognize that customer preferences can change, and personalization strategies should be adaptable.

EVENT-BASED MARKETING (April, 2023; Nov. 2018)

Event-based marketing is a strategy where businesses plan and execute marketing activities around specific events, either real-world occurrences or those created by the company. The goal is to capitalize on the attention and interest generated by these events to promote products or services. These events can be anything from holidays and cultural celebrations to product launches and industry conferences.

Types of Events:

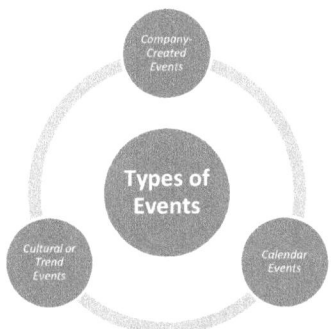

1. *Calendar Events*:
   Events that occur regularly, such as holidays (Christmas, New Year) or seasons, are used as opportunities for marketing promotions. For example, companies in various industries create marketing campaigns around Valentine's Day, offering themed products or services. For example, a restaurant might promote a special Valentine's Day menu.
2. *Company-Created Events*:
   Businesses can create their own events, like product launches, anniversaries, or special promotions, to generate buzz and engage customers. For example, many businesses capitalize on the shopping frenzy during Black Friday by offering special discounts and promotions, encouraging customers to make purchases during this event.
3. *Cultural or Trend Events*:
   Tapping into cultural trends or viral events to align marketing messages with what's currently capturing public attention.

Benefits of Event-Based Marketing:

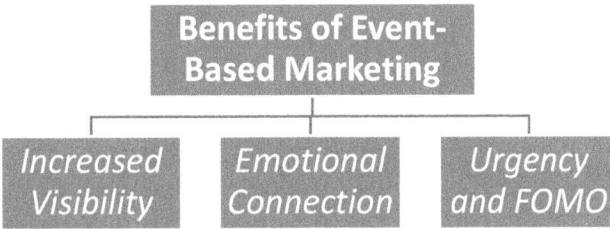

1. *Increased Visibility*:

Leveraging events allows businesses to tap into existing attention and gain visibility for their products or services.
2. *Emotional Connection*:
Events often evoke emotions, and aligning marketing messages with these emotions can create a stronger connection with the audience.
3. *Urgency and FOMO (Fear of Missing Out)*:
Limited-time promotions during events create a sense of urgency, encouraging customers to act to avoid missing out on special offers.

CRM AND CUSTOMER SERVICE

Customer service involves aiding and support to customers before, during, and after a purchase. It plays a crucial role in building and maintaining positive customer relationships.

Three key element of customer service:

There are three key elements of customer services which are:

1. Expand definition of service
2. Who are the customers
3. Develop a customer friendly approach

Expand definition of service:

Service refers to the intangible value provided to customers that goes beyond the physical product. It involves actions, efforts, and experiences aimed at satisfying customer needs and expectations.

Who are the customers

Customers are individuals or entities that purchase or use a product or service. In the context of customer service, anyone who interacts with a business is a potential customer, including buyers, users, and even those inquiring about products.

Develop a customer friendly approach

<u>Clear Communication</u>: Use simple and understandable language when communicating with customers. Avoid jargon and technical terms that might confuse them. For example, instead of saying, "Your query is in the queue," say, "We've received your question and will get back to you within 24 hours."

<u>Active Listening</u>: Pay attention to customer needs and concerns. Listening actively helps in understanding their requirements better. For example, if a customer expresses frustration, respond with understanding, "I hear you're frustrated, and I'm here to help resolve the issue."

<u>Empathy</u>: Put yourself in the customer's shoes to understand their perspective. Acknowledge their feelings and concerns. For example, I understand this must be frustrating for you. Let me see what I can do to make it right.

<u>Timely Response</u>: Respond to customer queries and issues promptly. Time is often critical in addressing concerns and creating a positive experience. For example, respond quickly to inquiries, "Thank you for reaching out! We're looking into this now and will get back to you shortly

<u>Problem Resolution</u>: Be proactive in solving problems. Take ownership of issues and work towards finding solutions rather than just providing excuses. For example, instead of saying, "We can't do that," say, "I understand the challenge. Let me explore some alternative solutions for you."

<u>Personalization</u>: Treat customers as individuals. Remember their preferences and personalize interactions whenever possible. For example, greet returning customers by name and inquire about their previous experiences. "Welcome back, [Customer Name]! How was your last experience with us?"

TECHNIQUES OF IMPROVING CUSTOMER SERVICE

Different techniques which are used to improve customer service are discussed as under:

1. Customer care software
2. Multimedia contact center deliveries
3. Call center and customer care
4. Call routing
5. Contact center sales support
6. Web-based self service
7. Customer satisfaction measurement
8. Call scripting
9. Cyber agents
10. Workforce management

CUSTOMER CARE SOFTWARE

Customer Care Software is a tool or set of tools designed to help businesses manage and improve their interactions with customers. It enables companies to streamline customer support, enhance communication, and provide a better overall experience. Few examples of customer care software are Zendesk, Freshdesk and HubSpot service Hub.

Zendesk offers a suite of customer service tools, including ticketing, live chat, and knowledge base.

Freshdesk provides a cloud-based customer support platform with features like ticketing, automation, and social media integration

Integrates with HubSpot's CRM, offering tools for customer feedback, live chat, and knowledge base management.

Key Features of Customer Care Software are:

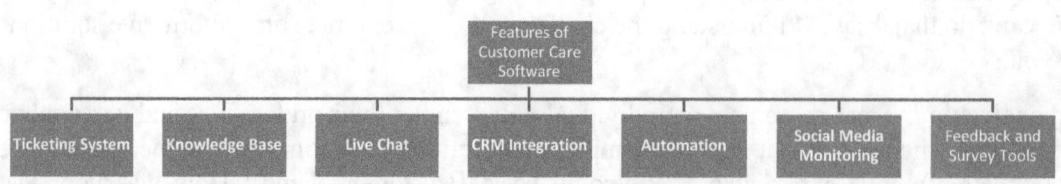

1. **Ticketing System**:
   A system that organizes and prioritizes customer inquiries. For example, a customer submits a request, and the software assigns it a unique ticket number for tracking.
2. **Knowledge Base**:
   A repository of information, FAQs, and solutions that customers can access. For example, customers can search the knowledge base for answers to common questions without contacting support.
3. **Live Chat**:
   Real-time messaging for instant customer support. For example, a customer visits a website and uses the live chat feature to get quick answers to their queries.
4. **CRM Integration**:
   Integration with Customer Relationship Management systems to centralize customer information. For example, customer care agents have access to a customer's purchase history and preferences.
5. **Automation**:
   Streamlining repetitive tasks and workflows. For example, automated email responses acknowledging receipt of a customer inquiry.
6. **Social Media Monitoring**:
   Tracking and responding to customer mentions on social media. For example, customer care software alerts the team when a customer posts a question on Twitter, allowing for a swift response.
7. **Feedback and Survey Tools**:
   Gathering customer feedback to measure satisfaction. For example, after a support interaction, customers receive a survey to rate their experience.

Benefits of Customer Care Software:

1. It reduces manual effort, automates tasks, and speeds up issue resolution.
2. It ensures a consistent level of service across all customer interactions.
3. It enhances communication channels between businesses and customers.
4. It provides insights into customer behavior and preferences.

CALL CENTRE AND CUSTOMER CARE (Nov. 2022)

Customer care involves all activities and interactions a company undertakes to address customer needs, concerns, and satisfaction throughout the customer journey. This task is mainly achieved with the help of call canters. A call canter is a centralized facility where customer service agents handle incoming and outgoing telephone calls from customers. It serves as a hub for customer interactions and issue resolution.

There are two basic classification for a call canter's function: inbound calls and outbound calls.

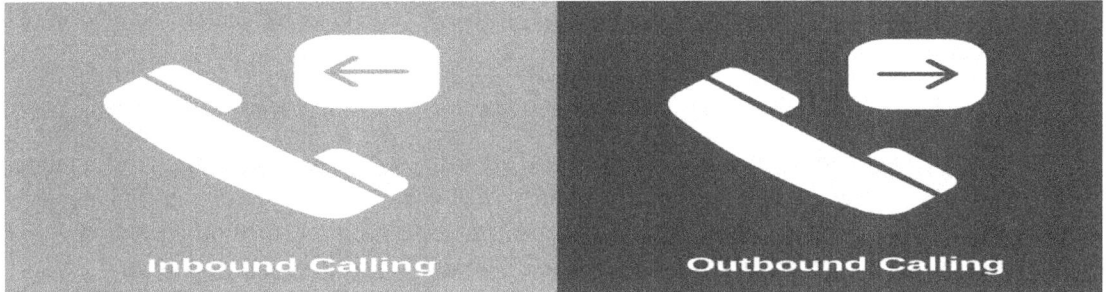

Inbound Calls:

Inbound calls refer to calls that are initiated by customers, clients, or other external parties seeking information, assistance, or support. The primary purpose of inbound calls is to address customer inquiries, resolve issues, provide information, or offer support based on the needs of the caller. Inbound calls are customer-driven, and the topics can vary widely based on customer needs. Calls may involve inquiries about products, services, billing, technical support, or general information. Agents focus on resolving customer issues promptly and efficiently. For example, a customer calls a tech support hotline because their internet connection is not working. The agent troubleshoots the issue, identifies the problem, and guides the customer through the necessary steps to restore the connection.

Outbound Calls:

Outbound calls are calls made by the call center or agents to external individuals or businesses. Unlike inbound calls, where customers initiate the contact, outbound calls involve the call center reaching out. Outbound calls are made for various purposes, including sales, marketing, customer follow-ups, surveys, and appointment reminders. Callers aim to engage the recipient in a conversation and convey a specific message. After a customer's interaction with the company, outbound calls may be made for follow-ups or to gather feedback. Outbound calls can also be used to schedule appointments or confirm existing ones. For example, a sales representative makes outbound calls to a list of potential customers to introduce a new product, highlight its features, and encourage purchases. The representative engages in conversations to address questions and ultimately close sales.

Components of call centre:

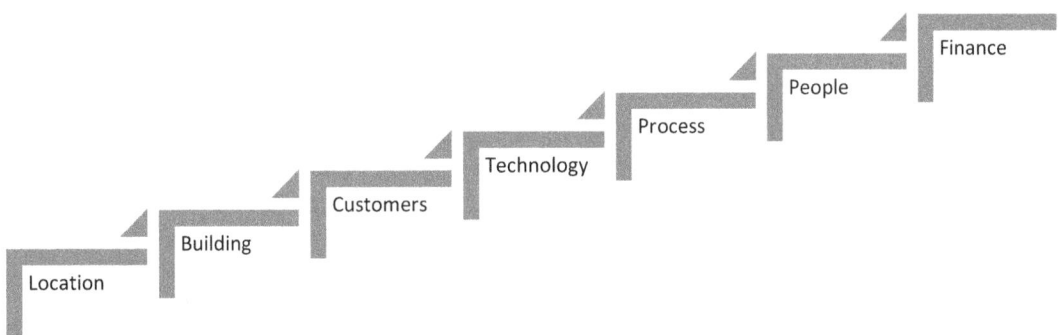

Location:

The location of a call center refers to the physical place where the center operates. It involves considerations such as accessibility, infrastructure, and proximity to potential employees and clients. For example, if a call center is located in a central business district, it can attract a

Building:

The building housing the call center is the physical structure where daily operations take place. It encompasses the layout, facilities, and security features. For example, the call center's building is designed with ergonomic workstations, meeting rooms for training sessions, and security measures like restricted access to ensure a conducive working environment.

Customers:

Customers are the individuals or businesses that contact the call center seeking assistance, information, or support regarding products or services. For example, in a telecommunication call center, customers may call in to inquire about their phone plans, request technical support, or resolve billing issues.

Technology:

Technology in a call center includes the tools and equipment used by agents to facilitate communication and support. This can include phones, headsets, computers, and software solutions. For example, agents utilize advanced customer relationship management (CRM) software, enabling them to access customer information swiftly and provide personalized assistance.

Process:

Processes in a call center refer to the step-by-step procedures followed to handle customer inquiries, manage workflows, and ensure the smooth operation of the center. For example, the call center has a well-defined process for logging customer issues, escalating problems to higher levels when necessary, and ensuring timely resolution to maintain customer satisfaction.

People:

People in a call center include the individuals involved in day-to-day operations, such as agents, supervisors, and managers. Effective training and communication skills are crucial for these roles. For example, agents undergo regular training sessions to enhance their communication skills, product knowledge, and problem-solving abilities, ensuring they can provide effective support to customers.

Finance:

Finance in a call center involves budgeting and financial considerations related to running operations, including technology upgrades, employee training, and overall operational costs. For example, allocating funds for technology upgrades ensures the call center stays current with the latest tools, contributing to operational efficiency and improved customer service.

Technology used in Call Canters:

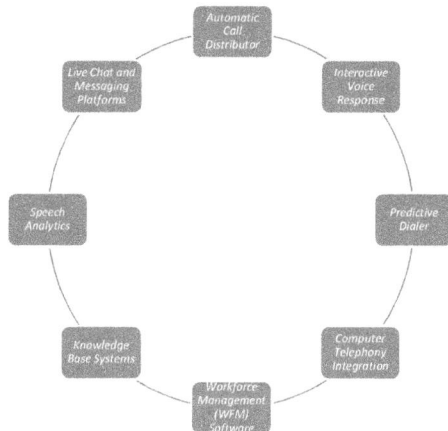

Automatic Call Distributor (ACD):

ACD is a system that routes incoming calls to the most appropriate agent based on predefined criteria. For example, when you call a customer service line and hear, "Press 1 for sales, press 2 for support," that's ACD in action.

Interactive Voice Response (IVR):

IVR systems use pre-recorded messages and voice recognition to guide callers to the right department or information. For example, "For account information, press 1. For billing inquiries, press 2."

Computer Telephony Integration (CTI):

CTI links phone systems with computer applications, allowing agents to access customer information during calls. For example, when an agent receives a call, the customer's details pop up on their screen automatically.

Predictive Dialer:

Predictive dialers automatically dial a list of phone numbers and connect agents to live calls, increasing efficiency. For example, outbound sales teams often use predictive dialers to maximize their calling time.

Speech Analytics:

Speech analytics uses technology to analyze and extract insights from recorded calls. For example, identifying customer sentiments or common issues through automated analysis of call recordings.

Live Chat and Messaging Platforms:

These platforms enable real-time communication between agents and customers through text-based chat. For example, LivePerson, Zendesk Chat, or Intercom provide live chat solutions for call centers.

Workforce Management (WFM) Software:

WFM helps optimize staff scheduling, ensuring the right number of agents are available at peak times. For example, Aspect, Verint, or Genesys provide WFM solutions for call centers.

Knowledge Base Systems:

Knowledge bases store information that agents can access to answer customer queries. For example, a searchable database containing product information, FAQs, and troubleshooting guides.

Examples of Call Center Solutions:

Few examples of call center are Ring Central Contact center, Genesys cloud, Talkdesk, etc.

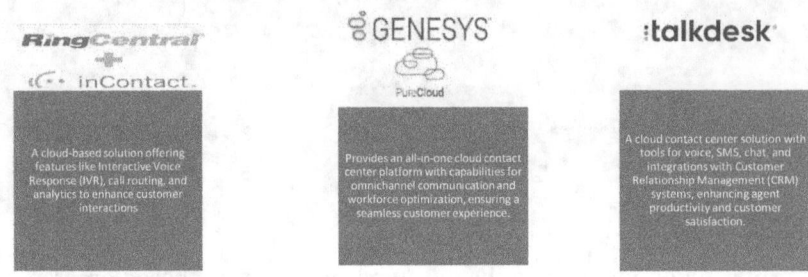

CALL ROUTING (Nov. 2018)

Call routing is a system that directs incoming calls to the most appropriate destination within a business or organization based on predetermined criteria. The goal is to efficiently connect callers to the right department, agent, or automated system.

Steps involved in call routing system:

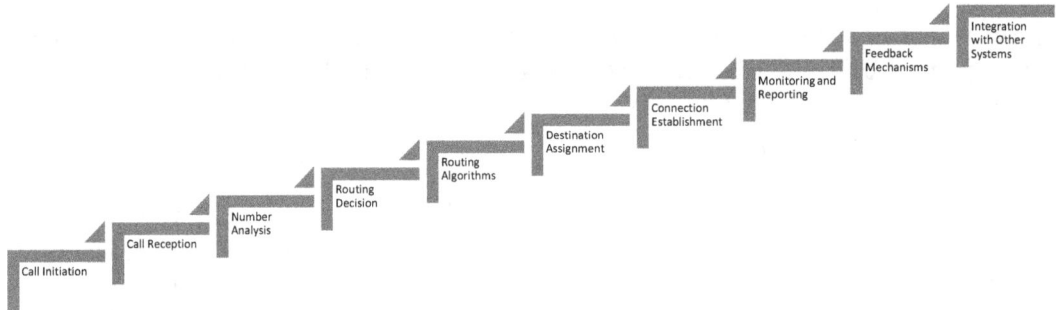

Call Initiation:

The process begins when someone initiates a phone call, either by dialing a number or through another communication channel like a VoIP (Voice over IP) application like Skype, WhatsApp, Pinger.

Call Reception:

The call routing system receives the incoming call. This system can be part of a traditional telephony infrastructure or a more modern VoIP (Voice over Internet Protocol) system.

Number Analysis:

The system analyzes the dialed number or other call parameters to determine the appropriate destination for the call. This analysis may include considering factors like the time of day, caller's location, or the nature of the call.

Routing Decision:

Based on the analysis, the system makes a routing decision to determine where the call should be directed. This decision can involve various criteria, such as routing to a specific department, individual, or geographical location.

Routing Algorithms:

Call routing systems use algorithms to make intelligent decisions. These algorithms can be simple, based on predetermined rules, or more sophisticated, using artificial intelligence to optimize routing based on historical data or real-time conditions.

Destination Assignment:

Once the routing decision is made, the call is directed to its designated destination. This could be an individual's desk phone, a call center agent, or a specific department.

Connection Establishment:

The call routing system establishes a connection between the caller and the destination. This may involve connecting through a traditional telephone network or using IP-based communication protocols.

Monitoring and Reporting:

Many call routing systems include monitoring and reporting features. These functionalities allow organizations to track call metrics, analyze call patterns, and optimize their routing strategies for better efficiency.

Fallback Mechanisms:

To enhance reliability, call routing systems often have fallback mechanisms in case the primary route is unavailable. This can involve rerouting calls or directing them to voicemail.

Integration with Other Systems:

In modern communication environments, call routing systems may integrate with other business systems, such as customer relationship management (CRM) software, to provide a seamless and personalized experience for callers.

Types of Call Routing:

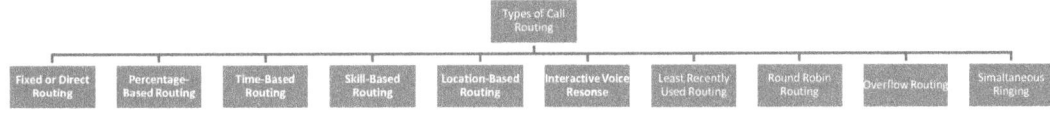

Fixed or Direct Routing:

Calls are routed directly to a predetermined destination without considering any dynamic factors. For example, a small business with a single phone line where all calls are directed to the owner's phone.

Percentage-Based Routing:

Description: Calls are distributed among multiple destinations based on a specified percentage allocation. For example, a customer support center might allocate 60% of incoming calls to one group of agents and 40% to another group to balance the workload.

Time-Based Routing:

Calls are routed differently based on the time of day, allowing for customized handling during business hours, after hours, or weekends. For example, calls to a sales department during business hours may go directly to sales representatives, while after hours, they are routed to voicemail or an on-call team.

Skill-Based Routing:

Calls are directed to individuals or teams with specific skills or expertise to handle the caller's needs. For example, in a technical support center, calls related to software issues may be routed to agents with expertise in software troubleshooting, while hardware issues go to another group.

Location-Based Routing:

Calls are directed to destinations based on the geographical location of the caller or the destination. For example, a multinational company may route calls from customers in different countries to specific call centers or regional offices based on the caller's location.

Interactive Voice Response (IVR):

A system that uses pre-recorded voice prompts and touch-tone keypad entries to route calls or provide information. For example, a bank's customer service hotline may use IVR to route callers to the appropriate department by asking them to select options based on their needs.

Least Recently Used (LRU) Routing:

Calls are directed to the agent who has been idle for the longest time, ensuring a fair distribution of workload. For example, in a call center, a call may be routed to the agent who has not recently handled a call to prevent overloading specific individuals.

Round Robin Routing:

Calls are distributed evenly among a group of agents, ensuring that each agent receives an equal share of incoming calls. For example, in a support center, calls are assigned to agents in a circular order, so each agent gets a turn to handle a call.

Overflow Routing:

Calls are initially directed to a primary destination, but if the line is busy or not answered, they are rerouted to a secondary destination. For example, calls to a customer service line might first go to the main support team, and if they are all busy, overflow to a backup team or voicemail.

Simultaneous Ringing:

Calls are sent to multiple destinations simultaneously, and the first to answer takes the call. For example, a sales hotline may simultaneously ring on the phones of multiple sales representatives, and the first one available answer the call.

Benefits of Call Routing:

1. Ensures calls are directed to the right destination quickly, reducing wait times for customers.

2. Improves customer experience by connecting them with the most qualified representative.
3. Distributes work evenly among agents or teams, optimizing workforce productivity.
4. Allows for personalized customer experiences by routing calls based on individual preferences or history.

CONTACT CENTER

A contact center is a centralized hub that manages communication between an organization and its customers, clients, or partners. It serves as a focal point for handling various forms of communication, including phone calls, emails, live chat, social media, and more.

Functions of a Contact Center:

1. Resolving customer issues, answering queries, and providing assistance.
2. Conducting sales activities, promoting products or services, and processing orders.
3. Assisting customers with technical issues or product-related problems.
4. Handling general inquiries and providing information about products or services.
5. Managing orders, tracking shipments, and handling returns.
6. Gathering customer feedback through surveys or post-interaction feedback.

Types of Contact Centers:

Inbound Contact Center:

Primarily handles incoming communications from customers seeking support, information, or assistance.

Outbound Contact Center:

Focuses on making outgoing calls, often for sales, lead generation, or follow-ups.

Blended Contact Center:

Combines both inbound and outbound functions, allowing agents to handle various types of communication.

Difference between Call Canter and Contact Canter

Basis	Call Center	Contact Center
Scope of Communication	Primarily focuses on handling voice-based communication, such as telephone calls.	Handles not only voice calls but also various other communication channels,

Basis	Call Center	Contact Center
		including email, live chat, social media, and more.
Communication Channels	The interaction is limited to verbal communication between agents and customers	It provides a more diverse range of options for customers to interact with the organization through email, live chat, social media, and more.
Integration of Channels	Integration with other communication channels may be limited.	Emphasizes an integrated approach, ensuring seamless communication across various channels.
Technological Infrastructure	Primarily relies on technologies that support voice communication, such as Interactive Voice Response (IVR) systems and Automatic Call Distributors (ACDs).	Utilizes a broader set of technologies, including omnichannel solutions, CRM integration, and artificial intelligence tools to facilitate communication across various channels.

CONTACT CENTER SALES SUPPORT

Contact Center Sales Support refers to the services and assistance provided by contact centers to support the sales process. It involves engaging with potential and existing customers to address inquiries, provide information, and guide them through the sales journey.

Functions of Contact Canter Sales Support:

1. Handling incoming calls from customers interested in products or services.
2. Proactively reaching out to potential customers for sales and promotions.
3. Providing detailed information about products or services to potential buyers.
4. Assisting customers in placing orders and managing the purchase process.
5. Suggesting additional products or upgrades to enhance the customer's purchase.
6. Addressing issues or concerns related to sales transactions.

WEB BASED SELF SERVICE (April, 2023; Nov. 2018)

Web-Based Self-Service refers to online platforms and tools that allow users to find information, perform tasks, and resolve issues independently without direct assistance from customer support. It empowers users to access resources and support through a company's website or application. Few key components of web-based self service are as under:

Knowledge Base:

A repository of articles which guides providing answers to common questions. For example, an IT company's website includes a knowledge base with articles on troubleshooting common software issues.

FAQ Sections:

Frequently Asked Questions section addressing common queries. For example, an e-commerce site has an FAQ page covering topics like order tracking, returns, and payment methods.

Tutorials and How-To Guides:

Step-by-step instructions for using products or services. For example, a software company's website offers tutorials on using specific features of their application.

Automated Chatbots:

Virtual assistants that interact with users to answer queries or guide them through processes. For example, an airline's website has a chatbot that assists users with flight bookings, baggage information, and FAQs.

User Forums and Communities:

Online spaces where users can ask questions, share experiences, and get advice from peers. For example, a gaming company hosts a community forum where players discuss game strategies, report issues, and share feedback.

Troubleshooting Tools:

Online tools that help users diagnose and resolve common problems. For example, a home appliance manufacturer's website has a diagnostic tool that guides users in identifying issues with their appliances.

Account Management:

Self-service portals for users to manage their accounts, update information, and track activities. For example, a banking website allows customers to log in and manage their accounts, view statements, and transfer funds independently.

CUSTOMER SATISFACTION MEASUREMENT

Customer Satisfaction Measurement is the process of evaluating and understanding how satisfied customers are with a company's products, services, or overall experience. It involves collecting feedback and data to gauge customer satisfaction levels. Following are some ways to measure customer satisfaction:

Surveys:

Sending out questionnaires or surveys to gather feedback directly from customers. For example, n online retailer emails customers a post-purchase survey to assess their satisfaction with the shopping experience and product quality.

Net Promoter Score (NPS):

A metric that measures the likelihood of customers recommending a company to others. For example, after a support interaction, a software company asks customers to rate on a scale of 0 to 10 how likely they are to recommend the product to a friend or colleague.

Customer Feedback Forms:

Forms on websites or in-store that allow customers to provide comments and suggestions. For example, a hotel provides feedback forms in guest rooms, encouraging visitors to share their experience and suggestions for improvement.

Social Media Listening:

Monitoring social media channels to understand customer sentiments and gather feedback. For example, a restaurant tracks mentions on social media platforms to assess customer reviews and respond to feedback.

Online Reviews:

Analyzing reviews on platforms like Yelp, Google Reviews, or industry-specific sites. For example, a mobile app developer reviews user feedback on the app store to understand user satisfaction and identify areas for improvement.

Customer Interviews:

Conducting one-on-one or group interviews to delve deeper into customer experiences. For example, an electronics manufacturer interviews a sample of customers to understand their perceptions of product quality, features, and customer support.

Benefits of Customer Satisfaction Measurement:

1. Pinpoints specific aspects of products or services that need enhancement.
2. Improves customer retention by addressing concerns and enhancing satisfaction.
3. Allows businesses to tailor their offerings to better meet customer expectations.
4. Provides valuable insights for making informed business decisions and strategic planning.

THE EXPECTATION-DISCONFIRMATION MODEL

The Expectation-Disconfirmation Model is a theoretical framework used to explain customer satisfaction. It suggests that customer satisfaction is influenced by the comparison between expectations and perceived performance or outcomes. The model proposes that satisfaction occurs when there is a positive disconfirmation, meaning that the perceived performance exceeds expectations

Expectations (E):

The customer's pre-consumption beliefs and anticipations about a product or service. Expectations can be shaped by past experiences, word of mouth, advertising, and other sources of information.

Perceived Performance (P):

The customer's assessment of the actual performance or outcome received from the product or service. Perceived performance is evaluated based on the customer's direct experience with the product or service.

Disconfirmation (D):

The comparison between expectations (E) and perceived performance (P).

Positive Disconfirmation: If perceived performance exceeds expectations, leading to higher satisfaction.

Negative Disconfirmation: If perceived performance falls below expectations, leading to dissatisfaction.

Customer Relationship Management

Satisfaction (S):

The overall positive or negative affective state resulting from the comparison of expectations and perceived performance.

Positive Satisfaction: When perceived performance is equal to or exceeds expectations.

Negative Satisfaction (Dissatisfaction): When perceived performance falls below expectations.

Mathematical Representation:

The model is often represented as $S=P-E$, where S is satisfaction, P is perceived performance, and E is expectations.

Positive values of S indicate positive satisfaction, while negative values indicate dissatisfaction.

The Expectation-Disconfirmation Model is widely used in marketing and customer satisfaction research to understand the psychological processes that influence customer perceptions and behaviors. Businesses can use insights from this model to tailor their strategies and improve overall customer satisfaction.

CALL-SCRIPTING (April, 2023)

Call scripting is the practice of providing a set of predefined and structured guidelines for customer service representatives or sales agents to follow during phone interactions with customers. These scripts outline the conversation flow, key points, and responses to ensure consistency and effectiveness. Some key components of call scripting are shown as under:

Introduction:

Clearly defined greetings and introduction phrases to set a positive tone. For example, "Hello, thank you for calling [Company Name]. My name is [Agent Name]. How may I assist you today?"

Problem Identification:

Questions and prompts to help identify the customer's issue or need. For example, "Could you please provide more details about the issue you're experiencing so that I can better assist you?"

Information Collection:

Structured prompts to gather necessary information from the customer. For example, "May I have your account number and some details about the nature of your inquiry?"

Solution Presentation:

Guidelines on presenting solutions or information in a clear and concise manner. For example, "Based on the information you provided, I recommend [specific solution or information]."

Handling Objections:

Prepared responses for common objections or concern customers may raise. For example, "I understand your concern. Let me assure you that [provide relevant information to address the concern]."

Closing the Call:

Scripted closing statements to end the call positively. For example, "Thank you for choosing [Company Name]. If you have any further questions, feel free to reach out. Have a great day!"

Benefits of Call Scripting:

1. Ensures that all customer interactions follow a standardized approach, maintaining consistency in service delivery.
2. Helps agents handle calls more efficiently by providing a structured framework.
3. Ensures that agents adhere to company policies, legal requirements, and best practices.
4. Aids in training new agents by providing a clear framework for customer interactions.
5. Facilitates monitoring and evaluation of calls for quality assurance purposes.

Challenges:

1. Over-reliance on scripts may lead to robotic interactions, lacking a personal touch.
2. Scripts may not cover every scenario, requiring agents to adapt based on the unique needs of each customer.

CYBER AGENTS

Cyber agents, in the context of technology and cybersecurity, refer to automated or intelligent systems designed to perform various tasks related to cybersecurity, including threat detection, prevention, and response. These agents are often powered by artificial intelligence (AI) and machine learning (ML) technologies.

Cyber agents attempt to pull together the best of both personalization and advanced technology. Cyber agent is given a personality- complete with voice and facial expressions. Often communicating with the web visitor by her first name.

In simple words, cyber agent is a person who is trying to help you virtually without seeing you or you seeing that person.

Benefits:

1. Cyber agents automate routine cybersecurity tasks, improving efficiency and response time.
2. Automated agents can scale to handle large and complex cybersecurity environments.
3. Cyber agents provide continuous monitoring, reducing the likelihood of overlooking security threats.
4. Machine learning algorithms enable cyber agents to adapt and improve their threat detection capabilities over time.

Challenges:

1. Cyber agents may generate false alarms, identifying normal behavior as a potential threat.
2. Cyber agents need regular updates to stay effective against new and sophisticated attacks.

WORKFORCE MANAGEMENT

Workforce Management involves the strategic planning, scheduling, and optimization of an organization's workforce to ensure that tasks are efficiently and effectively completed. It encompasses various processes, including staffing, scheduling, time and attendance tracking, and performance management. Certain key components of workforce management are discussed as under:

Staffing and Recruitment:

The process of acquiring and hiring employees with the right skills and qualifications. For example, a retail store uses workforce management to assess staffing needs during peak hours and hires seasonal workers accordingly.

Scheduling:

Creating and managing employee work schedules to ensure adequate coverage. For example, a call center uses workforce management software to create optimized schedules based on call volume patterns.

Time and Attendance Tracking:

Recording and monitoring employees' work hours and attendance. For example, an office uses a time-tracking system to record when employees clock in and out for accurate payroll processing.

Task Assignment:

Allocating specific tasks and responsibilities to employees based on their skills and availability. For example, in a manufacturing plant, workforce management ensures that workers with specific skills are assigned to tasks that match their expertise.

Performance Management:

Monitoring and evaluating employee performance to identify areas for improvement and recognize achievements. For example, a customer service center uses workforce management to track key performance indicators (KPIs) such as response time and customer satisfaction.

Forecasting and Planning:

Predicting future workforce needs based on historical data and business trends. For example, an e-commerce company uses workforce management tools to forecast the number of customer service representatives needed during holiday sales events.

Training and Development:

Providing ongoing training and development opportunities to enhance employees' skills. For example, a software company invests in workforce management programs to ensure that employees are trained on the latest technologies and methodologies.

Benefits of Workforce Management:

1. Ensures that the right people are in the right place at the right time, optimizing productivity.
2. Reduces labor costs by minimizing overtime and ensuring efficient resource utilization.
3. Improves employee satisfaction by creating fair schedules, considering preferences, and recognizing achievements.
4. Helps organizations adhere to labor laws and regulations related to working hours, breaks, and overtime.

5. Enables organizations to quickly adapt to changing business demands and market conditions.

Challenges of Workforce Management:

1. Workforce management can be complex, especially for large organizations with diverse workforce needs.
2. Implementing and integrating workforce management tools may require technological investments and adjustments.

CRM AND DATA MANAGEMENT (Nov. 2019; Nov. 2018)

Data Management involves the storage, and processing of consumer data to ensure its accuracy, security, and accessibility. The key components of data management are explained as under:

Data Quality Assurance:

Ensuring the accuracy and reliability of customer data through validation and verification processes. For example, regularly cleaning and updating customer contact information to avoid communication errors.

Data Security:

Implementing measures to protect customer data from unauthorized access and breaches. For example, encrypting sensitive customer information to safeguard it from potential cyber threats.

Data Integration:

Combining data from various sources to provide a comprehensive view of customer interactions. For example, integrating CRM data with marketing automation tools to align sales and marketing efforts.

Data Accessibility:

Ensuring that authorized users have timely access to accurate customer data. For example, implementing role-based access controls to restrict data access based on job responsibilities.

Data Governance:

Establishing policies and procedures for managing and using customer data responsibly. For example, creating guidelines on how customer data is collected, stored, and shared within the organization.

TYPES OF DATA (Nov. 2019; Nov. 2018)

Data can be categorized into various types based on its nature and usage in an organization. Here are detailed notes on different types of data:

Customer Relationship Management

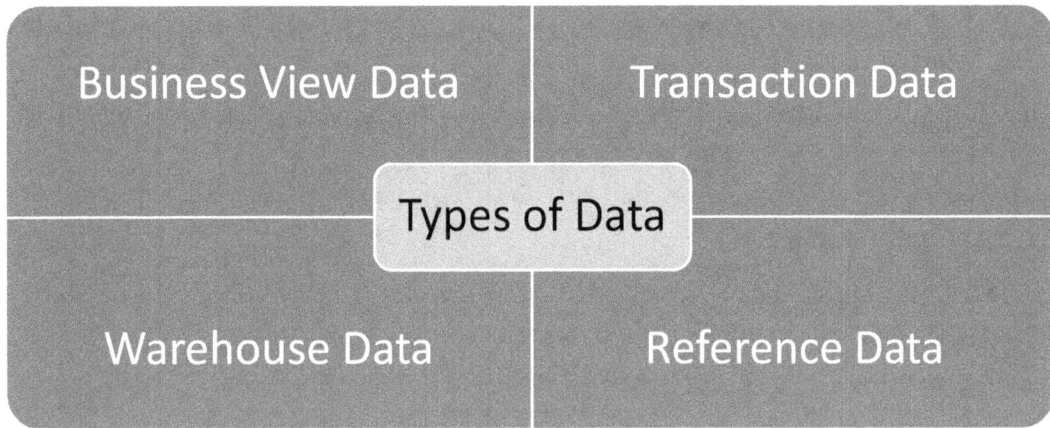

Transactional Data:

Transactional data records the day-to-day transactions of an organization. It is highly dynamic and represents the interactions within the business processes. It tends to be voluminous due to the large number of daily transactions, making it a significant component of operational databases. Transactional data forms the basis for decision-making processes within an organization. Analyzing this data helps in understanding sales patterns, customer behavior, and overall business performance. It is crucial for day-to-day operations, enabling the tracking and management of various business processes, such as order fulfillment, inventory management, and customer service.

Examples of Transactional Data:

Sales Transactions: These records detail the sale of products or services, including information such as item names, quantities, prices, and customer details.

Purchase Orders: Documents generated when a business requests goods or services from a supplier, specifying the items, quantities, and agreed-upon terms.

Invoices: Generated by a business to bill customers for goods or services rendered, containing details such as the amount due, payment terms, and transaction date.

Customer Interactions: Logs of interactions between the business and its customers, including communication history, service requests, and support interactions.

Reference Data:

Reference data is relatively stable and does not change frequently. It serves as a constant point of reference for interpreting and validating other types of data.

Reference data often follows standardized formats and codes, ensuring consistency across various business processes. Reference data is often centrally managed to maintain consistency across the organization, avoiding discrepancies in interpretation. Proper governance ensures that reference data is accurate, up-to-date, and aligned with business rules and regulations.

While relatively stable, reference data still requires careful management to accommodate updates or changes, especially in a global business environment. Ensuring consistency across systems and processes is crucial to prevent errors arising from discrepancies in reference data.

Examples of Reference Data:

<u>Country Codes</u>: Standardized codes assigned to different countries, facilitating international transactions and reporting.

<u>Currency Codes</u>: Codes assigned to different currencies, enabling consistent representation in financial transactions and reporting.

<u>Product Categories</u>: Classification codes for products or services, aiding in inventory management and sales categorization.

<u>Employee Types</u>: Categorization of employees based on roles, such as full-time, part-time, or contract.

Warehouse Data:

Warehouse data involves the consolidation of data from different operational sources into a central repository. This centralization facilitates unified reporting and analysis. Data in a warehouse is structured and optimized for analytical queries, providing a foundation for business intelligence and decision support. Warehouse data often includes historical records, allowing for trend analysis and long-term insights.

Examples of Warehouse Data:

<u>Aggregated Sales Data</u>: Summarized data that provides insights into overall sales performance, trends, and patterns.

<u>Summarized Financial Data</u>: Consolidated financial reports, enabling a high-level view of the organization's financial health.

<u>Historical Customer Data</u>: Records of customer interactions over time, supporting customer behavior analysis and segmentation.

Business View Data:

Business view data is tailored to the requirements of executives and managers, presenting information in a format that aligns with their decision-making processes. It focuses on providing clear and straightforward insights, often through visualizations like charts, graphs, and dashboards. Business view data offers a high-level perspective, emphasizing key performance indicators (KPIs) and critical metrics.

Examples of Business View Data:

<u>Key Performance Indicators (KPIs)</u>: Metrics that measure the performance of specific aspects of the business, such as revenue growth, customer satisfaction, or employee productivity.

<u>Dashboards</u>: Visual representations like charts, graphs that consolidate and display essential information, allowing decision-makers to quickly grasp the state of the business.

<u>Executive Summary Reports</u>: Concise reports that provide an overview of the organization's performance, typically highlighting achievements, challenges, and trends.

IDENTIFYING DATA QUALITY ISSUES (April, 2023; Nov. 2019, April, 2019)

Data quality issues refer to problems or shortcomings in the accuracy, completeness, consistency, and reliability of data. Identifying these issues is crucial for maintaining trustworthy and valuable data for business operations and decision-making.

Issues related to Data Quality:

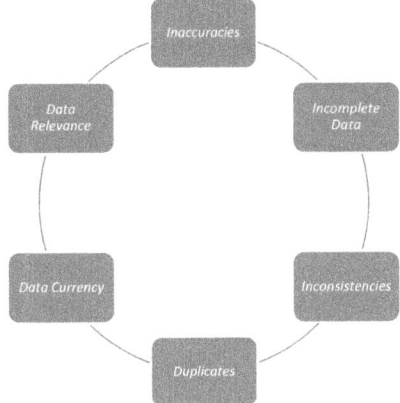

Inaccuracies:

Incorrect or outdated information that may lead to misguided decisions. For example, a customer's address in the database is outdated, leading to delivery issues.

Incomplete Data:

Missing or insufficient information that hinders a comprehensive understanding. For example, customer records without email addresses, limiting communication channels.

Inconsistencies:

Conflicting information within the dataset, causing confusion. For example, discrepancies in product pricing information across different databases.

Duplicates:

Multiple instances of the same data, potentially leading to errors and confusion. For example, duplicate customer entries in a CRM system, causing inaccuracies in reporting.

Data Currency:

Outdated information that no longer reflects the current state of the business or environment. For example, stock prices in a financial database not updated in real-time.

Data Relevance:

Information that is no longer applicable or necessary for current business needs. For example, retaining outdated product models in an inventory database.

Methods for Maintaining Data Quality:

Data Profiling:

Examining data to understand its structure, patterns, and potential anomalies. For example, profiling customer data to identify irregularities in the format of phone numbers.

Data Audits:

Regularly reviewing and validating data against predefined criteria. For example, auditing employee records to ensure completeness and accuracy.

Data Quality Tools:

Utilizing specialized software tools to automatically identify and address data quality issues. For example, implementing data quality software to scan and correct inconsistencies in a customer database.

User Feedback:

Gathering feedback from users who interact with the data to identify issues that may not be apparent through automated methods. For example, customer service representatives reporting discrepancies in customer contact details.

Data Governance Practices:

Implementing data governance policies and procedures to ensure consistent data quality. For example, establishing guidelines for entering and updating customer information in a CRM system.

Impact of Data Quality Issues:

1. Inaccurate or incomplete data may lead to misguided business decisions.
2. Poor data quality can result in inefficiencies and errors in day-to-day operations.
3. Inaccurate customer information can lead to service issues and dissatisfaction.
4. Violations of data protection regulations may occur if data quality issues compromise privacy or security.

PLANNING AND GETTING INFORMATION QUALITY

Planning and ensuring information quality involve strategic efforts to proactively manage, maintain, and enhance the quality of data and information within an organization. It encompasses processes, methodologies, and technologies aimed at achieving accurate, consistent, and reliable information. Following are the six stages that helps to plan and get qualitative information:

Data Profiling:

Data profiling involves analyzing and understanding the structure, content, and quality of your data. The process of data profiling involves following steps:

- Identify data sources.
- Examine data types, patterns, and relationships.
- Evaluate data consistency and accuracy.

For example, suppose you're working with a customer database. Data profiling might reveal inconsistencies in how addresses are recorded (e.g., varying formats) or missing information in certain entries.

Data Control:

Implementing measures to control and manage the quality of data throughout its lifecycle. Thus, it establish data governance policies, define roles and responsibilities for data management and finally implement access controls and security measures. For example, create policies that specify who has permission to modify certain types of data, ensuring that only authorized personnel can make changes.

Data Integration:

Combining data from different sources to provide a unified view. It also ensure consistency in integrated data. For example, integrating sales data from both online and in-store transactions to have a comprehensive view of overall sales performance.

Data Augmentation:

It enhances existing datasets with additional information. For example, adding demographic information to a customer database to better understand the target audience and tailor marketing strategies.

Monitor Data and Assign Ownership:

Regularly monitoring data quality and assigning responsibility for data ownership. For example, using automated tools to monitor for data anomalies and assigning a data steward to oversee the accuracy and completeness of customer contact information.

Train Users and Commit to a Data Quality Process:

Provide training to users who handle or interact with data and establish a formalized process for continuous data quality improvement. For example, training sales representatives on the proper way to input customer data to maintain consistency and accuracy in the CRM system.

USING TOOLS TO MANAGE THE DATA

Using tools to manage data involves the utilization of software applications and technologies designed to handle, organize, analyze, and optimize data throughout its lifecycle. These tools are instrumental in ensuring data quality, security, and accessibility. Few categories of data management tools are:

Data Integration Tools:

Tools that facilitate the combining of data from different sources into a unified view. For example, Talend, an open-source data integration tool, allows users to connect, transform, and manage data across various systems.

Data Quality Tools:

Tools designed to assess, monitor, and improve the quality of data by identifying and correcting errors or inconsistencies. For example, Informatica Data Quality provides capabilities to profile, cleanse, and standardize data to ensure high-quality information.

Data Governance Tools:

Tools that support the establishment and enforcement of data governance policies and practices. For example, Collibra is a data governance platform that helps organizations define and manage data policies, standards, and workflows.

Master Data Management (MDM) Tools:

Tools designed to manage and synchronize master data, ensuring consistency and accuracy across an organization. For example, IBM InfoSphere Master Data Management helps organizations manage and maintain a single, accurate view of master data.

Data Warehousing Tools:

Tools that enable the storage, retrieval, and analysis of large volumes of data for reporting and business intelligence purposes. For example, Snowflake is a cloud-based data warehousing platform that allows organizations to store and analyze data at scale.

Data Visualization Tools:

Tools that convert complex data sets into visual representations, making it easier to interpret and analyze. For example, Tableau is a popular data visualization tool that allows users to create interactive and shareable dashboards.

DATA ANALYSIS (April, 2023; Nov. 2022; April, 2019)

Data analysis is the process of inspecting, cleaning, transforming, and modeling data to discover useful information, draw conclusions, and support decision-making. It involves examining and interpreting data to extract meaningful insights, identify patterns, and make informed decisions. Data analysis can be performed using various methods, statistical techniques, and software tools to uncover trends, correlations, and relationships within datasets. The ultimate goal of data analysis is to turn raw data into actionable knowledge that can inform business strategies, scientific research, or other decision-making processes. In CRM, there are many ways of analysing the data which are explained below:

DATA MINING

Data mining is the process of discovering patterns, trends, correlations, or meaningful insights by analyzing large datasets. It involves extracting useful and previously unknown information from data to support decision-making, identify relationships, and make predictions. Data mining is a multidisciplinary field that incorporates techniques from statistics, machine learning, database management, and artificial intelligence. Challenges in data mining include dealing with large volumes of data, selecting appropriate algorithms, addressing biases, and ensuring the ethical use of data.

Various techniques used in data mining are:

Association Rule Mining:

Discovering relationships between variables in the form of "if-then" rules.

Classification:

Assigning data to predefined categories based on its features.

Regression Analysis:

Predicting numerical values based on historical data.

Clustering:

Grouping similar data points together based on certain criteria.

Anomaly Detection:

Identifying unusual patterns or outliers in the data.

ONLINE ANALYTICAL PROCESSING (OLAP):

Online Analytical Processing, or OLAP, is a category of software tools and technologies that enable users to interactively analyze and explore multidimensional data. It facilitates complex and strategic analysis of large datasets, allowing users to gain insights from different perspectives. The various features of OLAP system is as follows:

Multidimensionality:

OLAP systems organize data into multidimensional cubes, where each dimension represents a specific aspect or attribute of the data. For example, in a sales cube, dimensions may include time, products, and geographic regions.

Interactivity:

Users can interactively navigate and explore data, drilling down into detailed information or rolling up to higher-level summaries. For example, a user can drill down from yearly sales to quarterly, monthly, and daily sales figures.

Data Aggregation:

OLAP allows the aggregation of data at various levels of granularity, supporting both high-level overviews and detailed analysis. For example, aggregating sales data to show total revenue or breaking it down to show revenue by product category.

Calculation and Formulas:

OLAP systems support the creation of calculated measures and formulas for deriving new insights or performance indicators. For example, calculating profit margins based on sales and cost data within the OLAP cube.

Flexibility:

Users can easily pivot, slice, and dice data to view it from different angles and dimensions, providing flexibility in analysis. For example, pivoting a sales cube to view revenue by product category instead of by geographic region.

Fast Query Response:

OLAP systems are optimized for fast query response times, allowing users to retrieve and analyze data quickly. For example, instantly generating reports and visualizations even with large datasets.

Example: Imagine a retail company that operates in different regions, sells various products, and tracks sales data over time.

OLAP Cube Dimensions:

Time Dimension:

Hierarchy: Year > Quarter > Month > Day

Product Dimension:

Hierarchy: Category > Subcategory > Product

Geographic Dimension:

Hierarchy: Country > Region > City

Measures:

Sales Revenue

Units Sold

Profit Margin

CLICKSTREAM ANALYSIS:

Clickstream analysis involves the examination and interpretation of user interactions with a website or digital platform. It analyzes the sequence of clicks, page views, and other actions taken by users, providing insights into their behavior and preferences. The main components of clickstream data are:

Page Views:

Records the pages a user visits during their session on a website or application.

Clicks:

Captures the specific links or elements clicked by the user, indicating their navigation path.

Timestamps:

Records the time when each action occurs, allowing for the analysis of user behavior over time.

Customer Relationship Management

Referrers:

Indicates the source from which the user arrived at the website, providing insights into marketing effectiveness.

Session Duration:

Measures the time a user spends on the website during a single session.

Example: a user lands on the homepage, clicks on a product category, views several product pages, adds an item to the cart, and finally makes a purchase. Clickstream analysis reveals the most common paths users take, helping optimize website navigation.

Benefits of Clickstream Analysis:

1. Improves website design and navigation based on user behavior, enhancing the overall user experience.
2. Identifies and addresses bottlenecks in the user journey, leading to increased conversion rates.
3. Informs content strategy by highlighting popular topics and areas of user interest.
4. Enables the assessment of the effectiveness of different marketing channels and campaigns.
5. Provides data for tailoring content and recommendations to individual user preferences.

PERSONALIZATION:

Personalization in the context of digital experiences involves tailoring content, products, or services to meet the unique preferences and needs of individual users. It aims to create a more relevant and engaging user experience by delivering personalized recommendations, content, and interactions. The main features of personalization are:

User Data:

Personalization relies on collecting and analyzing user data, including preferences, behavior, and demographics.

Recommendation Engines:

Algorithms and systems that analyze user data to suggest personalized content, products, or actions.

Behavioral Tracking:

Monitoring and analyzing user interactions and behaviors to understand preferences and patterns.

User Profiles:

Creating profiles for individual users based on their preferences, purchase history, and engagement with the platform.

Example, an online retailer analyzes a user's past purchase history and browsing behavior to recommend products tailored to their interests. For example, suggesting additional items based on a user's recent purchase or browsing history.

Benefits of Personalization:

1. Personalized experiences capture user attention and encourage longer and more meaningful interactions.
2. Meeting individual preferences and needs leads to higher customer satisfaction and loyalty.
3. Personalized recommendations and content increase the likelihood of users taking desired actions, such as making a purchase.
4. Targeted and personalized marketing efforts are more efficient, reducing wasted resources on irrelevant outreach.
5. Leveraging user data for personalization allows businesses to make data-driven decisions and continually improve the user experience.

COLLABORATIVE FILTERING:

Collaborative filtering is a recommendation technique that predicts a user's preferences based on the preferences and behaviors of other users. It relies on the idea that users who have similar preferences in the past are likely to have similar preferences in the future.

Types of Collaborative Filtering:

User-Based Collaborative Filtering:

Recommends items based on the preferences of users who are similar to the target user. For example, if User A and User B have similar preferences and User A likes a movie, User B is likely to receive recommendations for the same movie.

Item-Based Collaborative Filtering:

Recommends items that are similar to those liked by the target user. For example, if User X likes a particular book, the system recommends other books that users with similar preferences have liked.

Benefits of Collaborative Filtering:

1. Provides personalized recommendations based on user behavior and preferences.
2. Recommends items that users with similar tastes have liked, facilitating the discovery of new content.
3. Adapts to changing user preferences over time, making it suitable for dynamic recommendation scenarios.

DATA REPORTING (April, 2023)

Data reporting in Customer Relationship Management (CRM) involves the collection, analysis, and interpretation of data to gain insights into customer behavior, sales performance, and overall business efficiency. The primary goal of data reporting is to analyze customer data to improve customer satisfaction, loyalty, and overall relationship management. It also helps in understanding customer behavior, preferences, and trends, allowing for personalized and targeted interactions.

Challenges in CRM Data Reporting:

Data Silos:

Integration challenges may arise when attempting to combine data from different sources.

Customer Relationship Management

Privacy Concerns:

Ensure compliance with data protection regulations when reporting on customer information.

Adoption and Training:

Challenges may emerge in getting teams to adopt and effectively use CRM reporting tools.

QUESTIONS

Multiple choice questions (MCQs):

a) _____ is one of the most useful tools in a salesperson's toolbox when it comes to increasing sales volume per customer.
(i)Customer Management (ii) Up-selling (iii) Cross-selling (iv) Direct- selling

b) Offering a greater quantity for a slightly higher price is an example of _____. (Oct. 18)
(i)Cross-selling (ii) Up-selling (iii) Personalization (iv) Bancassurance

c) _____ reflects "the state of mind that customers have about a company and its products or services when their expectations have been met or exceeded.
(i)Customer Management (ii) Customer Retention (iii) Customer Acquisition (iv) Customer Attrition

d) _____ is crucial to maintain and grow customer relationships to sustain profitable growth.
(i) Customer Management (ii) Customer. Retention (iii) Customer Acquisition (iv) Customer Attrition

e) _____ means providing a quality product or service that satisfies the needs/wants of a customer and keeps them coming back.
(i)Customer representative (ii) Customer Service (iii) Customer Survey (iv) Customer EPOS

f) _____ is an electronic system whereby at checkout point data is been collected customers will get served quicker.
(i)E-CRM (ii) Customer Service (iii) PoS (iv) EPOS (Electronic point of sale)

g) _____ allows the organization to contact its customers in the medium of their choice - voice, e-mail, web chat, fax, SMS.
(i)E-CRM (ii) Multimedia contact centre (iii) PoS (iv) EPOS (Electronic point of sales)

h) _____ of the call centre is critical in terms of the cost of the building and also the ability to recruit and retain employees to work in the centre.
(i)Location (ii) Customer (iii) Technology (iv) Process

i) Choice of _____ depends on the size and nature of business.
(i)Location (ii) Customer (iii) Technology (iv) Process

j) _____ are the most critical asset in a call centre as it is they who deliver the business performance.
(i)Location (ii) People (iii) Customer (iv) Process

k) _____ exists when perception > expectation. (Oct. 18)
(i)Customer satisfaction (ii) Customer dissatisfaction (iii) Customer delight (iv) Customer engagement

l) The process of forecasting contact centre workload and then scheduling agents to handle the workload is known as _____ .(Oct. 18)
(i)CRM (ii) Call scripting (iii) Workforce management (iv) Relationship marketing management

Customer Relationship Management

m) _____ is a central point in an enterprise from which all customer contacts are maintained such as e-mails, newsletters, chats, etc. (Oct. 18)
   (i)Call centre (ii) Contact centre (iii) Customer care centre (iv) Development centre

n) A business strategy designed to optimise profitability, revenue and satisfaction. (May 19)
   (i)producer (ii) distributor (iii) consumer (iv) government

o) _____ plays a significant role to generate revenue, control costs and mitigate risks.
   (i)Data Profiling (ii) Data Control (iii) Data management (iv) Data Integration

p) _____ is generated from data warehouse. Business views are calculations or summaries compared over some time.
   (i)Transactional Data (ii) Reference Data (iii) Business view Data (iv) Data Integration

q) _____ is the data without which you cannot do any transactions and is mandatory for every organization.
   (i)Transactional Data (ii) Reference Data (iii) Business view Data (iv) Data Integration

r) _____ refers to the data that is created and updated within the operational systems.
   (i)Transactional Data (ii) Reference Data (iii) Business view Data (iv) Data Integration

s) _____ resulting in a single source of "truth" and making it easier for end-users to access information.
   (i)Data Profiling (ii) Data Control (iii) Data management (iv) Data Integration

t) _____ is a method of recommending product or services to visitors on websites. (Oct. 18)
   (i)Clickstream analysis (ii) Online analytical process (iii) Collaborative filtering (iv) Traffic analysis

u) OLAP means the on-line _____ processing. (May 19)
   (i)analytical (ii) administrative (iii) adjustment (iv) affiliation

v) Data _____ is the process of collecting and submitting data to the entitled authorities. (May 19)
   (i)assembling (ii) recording (iii) reporting (iv) reversing

Answers:- (a - iii), (b - ii), (c - ii), (d - iv), (e - ii), (f - iv), (g - ii), (h - iii), (i - iii), (j - iii), (k - i), (l - in), (m - ii), (n-iii), (o - iii), (p - ii), (q - ii), (r - i), (s - iv). (t -i), (u -i), (v -i)]

Fill in the blanks:

(a) The state of mind that customers have about a company and its products or services when their expectations have been met or exceeded is known as _____.

(b) _____ ties to both financial and social incentives.

(c) There are _____ levels of retention strategies.

(d) _____ bond deals with Mass customization and customer intimacy.

(e) _____ customers have every intention of continuing to do business with you and they have a positive attitude toward your company.

(f) A _____ desk is situated mostly near the entrance to the store.

(g) _____ marketing is also customer-specific marketing.

(h) Customer _____ means providing a quality product or service that satisfies the needs/wants of a customer and keeps them coming back.

(i) Modern CRM theory refers to the idea of _____ the customer'.

(j) A _____ is a professional who works either directly with or directly for the customers and prospective customers of a given company.

(k) _____ is an electronic system whereby at checkout point data is been collected customers will get served quicker.

(l) Research shows that companies can increase profitability by _____ percent if they can just retain 5 percent more of their profitable customers per year.

Customer Relationship Management

(m) _____ starts with the ability to listen to the customer and find out through polite questioning what he/she needs or wants.

(n) _____ refers to the collection of raw facts and figures.

(o) _____ refers to the data that is created and updated within the operational systems.

(p) _____ is the data that will describe the type of object, like name, description, cost, length and dimensions of the object. It is one-time data.

(q) _____ is generated from data warehouse. Business views are calculations or summaries compared over some time.

Answers:- (a) Customer Retention, (b) Social bond retention strategy, (c) Four, (d) Customization bonds, (e) Truly Loyal, U) Customer service, (g) Event-based marketing, (h) Service, (i) Integrating, (j) customer service representative, (k) EPOS, (l) 100, (m) Customer service, (n) Data, (o) Transactional data, (p) Reference Data, (q) Business View Data]

True or False:

(a) Up-selling is one of the most useful tools in a salesperson's toolbox when it comes to increasing sales volume per customer.

(b) Cross-selling involves the increase of order volume either by the sales of more units of the same purchased item, or the upgrading into a more expensive version of the purchased item.

(c) Customer retention requires attention to customer details.

(d) Customer retention reflects "the state of mind that customers have about a company and its products or services when their expectations have been met or exceeded.

(e) Customer attrition is crucial to maintain and grow customer relationships to sustain profitable growth.

(f) Event-based marketing is also known as trigger marketing. (Oct. 18)

(g) Customer engagement is not a customer retention strategy. (Oct. 18)

(h) Personalization consists of tailoring a service or product to accommodate specific individual needs. (Oct. 18)

(i) Effective customer segmentation is only possible through a multi-dimensional customer view.

(j) Research shows that companies can increase profitability by 100 if they can just retain 10 percent more of their profitable customers per year.

(k) Internet self-service reduces support costs by increasing call centre volume.

(l) Good customer service results in consumer satisfaction and returns customers and growth in business.

(m) Customer Survey starts with the ability to listen to the customer and find out through polite questioning what he/she needs or wants.

(n) Customer Service is the interaction between a customer and the company, usually via traditional channels like phone or email.

(o) An EPOS system comprises computer hardware, peripherals, and EPOS software ideally suited to the point of the sales environment.

(p) Call routing helps to save expensive man-hours. (May 19)

(q) Accurate information and reports are the lifeblood of an effective sales force.

(r) Data control is all about understanding your data.

(s) Data profiling is all about achieving data accuracy and ensuring the right users have access to the right information, which also means blocking access, as needed.

(t) Data integration results in a single source of "truth" and making it easier for end-users to access information.

(u) Data Augmentation can help reduce the manual intervention required to developed meaningful information and insight into business data.

(v) Data profiling helps to plan and get qualitative information. (Oct. 18)

(w) Data reporting is a written script that has correct wordings and assists an agent in handling a contact. (Oct. 18)

(x) Usually, the information is the raw material of CRM. (May 19)

Answers:- (a) False, (b) False, (c) True, (d) True, (e) True, (f) True, (g) False, (h) True, (i) True, (j) False, (k) False, (l) True, (m) False, (n) True, (o) True, (p) True, (q) True, (r) False, (s) False, (t) True, (u) True, (v) True, (w) True, (x) True

Match the following:

Group 'A'		Group 'B'	
(a)	Financial bonds	(i)	Low price to make huge purchases
(b)	Social bonds	(ii)	Strategic changes
(c)	Customization bonds	(iii)	Personalization incentives
(d)	Structural bonds	(iv)	Financial and social incentives
(e)	ACD	(v)	Flexible software
(f)	IVR	(vi)	Customer contact channels with the computer
(g)	CTI	(vii)	The first point in the customer center
(h)	ICR	(viii)	Front end
(i)	Data profiling	(ix)	Achieving data accuracy and ensuring the right users have access to the right information
(j)	Data control	(x)	Data created and updated within the operational systems
(k)	Data integration	(xi)	Adds value to base data
(l)	Data augmentation	(xii)	Integrate data in one system
(m)	Database marketing	(xiii)	Identify potential problems with current data
(n)	Transactional data	(xiv)	Data without which you cannot do any transactions and is mandatory for every organization
(o)	Reference data	(xv)	Unique segments in the database

Answers:- (a – i), (b – iv), (c- iii), (d – ii), (e – vii), (f – viii), (g – vi), (h – v), (i – xiii), (j – ix), (k – xii), (l – xi), (m – xv), (n – x), (o – xiv)

long answer type questions:

Q. Explain call scripting. (April, 2023)

Q. Explain behaviour prediction. (April, 2023)

Q. Describe the types of data analysis. (April, 2023; Nov. 2022; April, 2019)

Q. Explain the concept of data reporting. (April, 2023)

Q. Explain the concept of event-based marketing and web-based self-service. (April, 2023; Nov. 2018)

Q. What are the quality issues identified in the data? (April, 2023; Nov. 2019, April, 2019)

Q. What do you mean by brand switching? Discuss the reasons for the same. (Nov. 2022)

Q. Explain components of call centers. (Nov. 2022)

Q. Explain customer retention, write in detail about the need for customer retention. (Nov. 2022; Nov. 2019)

Q. What is data management and explain its different types. (Nov. 2019; Nov. 2018)

Q. Discuss customer profitability and value modelling. (Nov. 2019; Nov. 2018)

Q. Explain the concept of cross-selling and up-selling. (April, 2019)

Q. What is call routing. Explain different techniques of call-routing. (Nov. 2018)

UNIT 3: CRM STRATEGY, PLANNING, IMPLEMENTATION AND EVALUATION

- ✓ Customer value
- ✓ Customer value management (CVM)
- ✓ Customer value management (CVM) framework
- ✓ Customer profit chain: satisfaction, loyalty. Retention and profits:
- ✓ CRM strategy
- ✓ The CRM (customer relationship management) strategy cycle:
- ✓ Planning of CRM
- ✓ Business to business (B2B) CRM
- ✓ Market information vs market intelligence
- ✓ Cross border b2b relationship with intermediaries
- ✓ Sales and CRM
- ✓ Salesforce automation
- ✓ Activity management
- ✓ Sales territory management
- ✓ Contact management
- ✓ Lead management
- ✓ Configuration management
- ✓ Knowledge management
- ✓ CRM implementation
- ✓ CRM evaluation
- ✓ Service quality in achieving customer satisfaction:
- ✓ Service quality gap
- ✓ Importance of research for improving service quality:
- ✓ Walker customer loyalty matrix
- ✓ 3e's measures of CRM: (efficiency, effectiveness and employee change)

> ✓ Questions

CUSTOMER VALUE (April, 2023; April, 2019)

Customer value is the benefit a customer gets from using a product or service compared to the cost of obtaining and using it. For example, Apple's focus on sleek design, user-friendly interface, and constant innovation creates value for customers, justifying the premium price.

Calculation of customer value depends upon two components: benefits and costs.

Benefits: What the customer gains.

Costs: What the customer gives up (money, time, effort).

For example, a smartphone with a high-quality camera provides value for customers who love taking pictures without carrying a separate camera.

Importance of Understanding Customer Value:

1. When customers feel they get more value than they paid for, they're satisfied.
2. Satisfied customers are more likely to return and make repeat purchases.
3. Happy customers share their positive experiences, bringing in new customers.
4. Listen to customer feedback to understand what they appreciate or find lacking.
5. Conduct surveys to gather data on customer preferences and expectations.
6. Stay updated on market trends to align your offerings with changing customer needs.
7. Regularly assess and improve products or services based on customer feedback.

CUSTOMER VALUE MANAGEMENT (CVM)

CVM is a strategy, businesses use to maximize the value customers get from their products or services, fostering loyalty and long-term relationships. In involves understanding customers needs in terms of identifying customers value and prioritize those aspects and further consistently provide products or services that meet or exceed customer expectations. For example, Netflix understands that customers value personalized content. Their recommendation algorithm suggests shows based on viewing history, enhancing the user experience. Amazon Prime offers a combination of fast shipping, exclusive content, and additional services to make the subscription valuable for customers.

Importance of CVM:

1. By consistently delivering value, businesses keep customers coming back.
2. Providing unique and superior value sets a business apart from competitors.
3. Satisfied customers are more likely to make repeat purchases, contributing to long-term profitability.

Strategies for Implementing CVM:

1. Understand that different customer segments may value different things. Tailor the approach accordingly.

Customer Relationship Management

2. Establish mechanisms for gathering customer feedback and use it to improve products or services.
3. Regularly reassess customer needs and adapt strategies to meet evolving expectations.
4. Embrace innovation to stay ahead in delivering value.

CUSTOMER VALUE MANAGEMENT (CVM) FRAMEWORK:

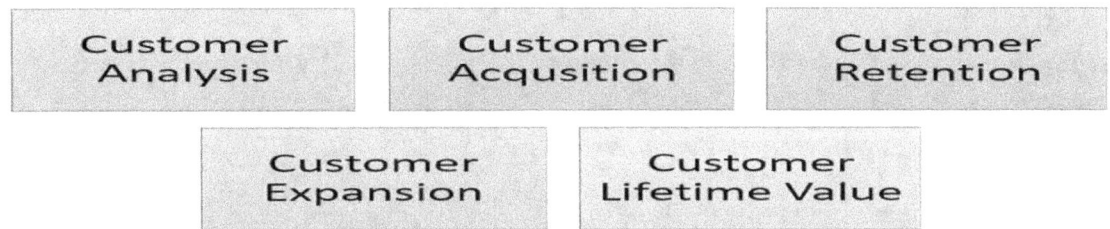

Customer Analysis:

Understanding who your customers are, what they need, and how they behave. For example, an online clothing store analyzes data to find that their customers are mostly young adults who prefer trendy and affordable fashion.

Customer Acquisition:

Bringing in new customers to try your product or service. surveys, feedback, and data analytics can be used to understand customer preferences. Promotions, discounts, or free trials may be offered to attract new customers. For example, a coffee shop offers a "Buy One Get One Free" promotion for first-time customers, attracting new people to try their coffee.

Customer Retention:

Keeping existing customers satisfied and coming back for more. Excellent customer service, loyalty programs, and personalized experiences can be provided to retain the customers. For example, a software company provides excellent customer support and regular updates to retain customers and prevent them from switching to a competitor.

Customer Expansion:

Increasing the value, you provide to existing customers and encouraging them to spend more. New products or services, upsell/cross-sell, and create loyalty tiers may be introduced to expand customer base. For example, a gym introduces new fitness classes or personalized training sessions to encourage current members to upgrade their memberships.

Customer Life Time Value:

Customer Lifetime Value (CLV or CLTV) is a metric that represents the total revenue a business can reasonably expect to earn from a customer throughout their entire relationship. It is a crucial metric for businesses to assess the long-term value of acquiring and retaining customers. CLV helps businesses make informed decisions about customer acquisition costs, marketing strategies, and overall customer relationship management. The formula for calculating Customer Lifetime Value is:

$$CLV = \left(\frac{\text{Average Purchase Value} \times \text{Purchase Frequency}}{\text{Churn Rate}} \right)$$

Where:

Average Purchase Value: The average amount of money a customer spends per transaction.

Purchase Frequency: How often a customer makes a purchase within a given time period.

Churn Rate: The rate at which customers stop doing business with the company (1 - Retention Rate).

For example:

Let's say a subscription-based software company calculates the CLV for one of its customer segments:

Average Purchase Value: $50

Purchase Frequency: 2 purchases per month

Churn Rate: 10% (Retention Rate: 90%)

$$CLV = \left(\frac{\$50 \times 2}{0.10}\right) = \$1,000$$

In this example, the company can expect to earn $1,000 from a customer in this segment over the course of the relationship.

Importance of CVM Framework:

1. It helps businesses see the complete picture of their customer relationships.
2. Balancing acquisition, retention, and expansion optimizes the overall value each customer brings to the business.

Real-Life Example of CVM Framework: (Amazon Prime)

Customer Analysis:

Amazon understands that customers value fast shipping and exclusive content.

Customer Acquisition:

They offer a free trial to attract new subscribers.

Customer Retention:

The membership includes benefits like streaming services and discounts, encouraging customers to stay.

Customer Expansion:

Amazon constantly adds new features like Prime Day, expanding the value for existing members.

CUSTOMER PROFIT CHAIN: SATISFACTION, LOYALTY. RETENTION AND PROFITS: (April, 2023)

Customer Relationship Management

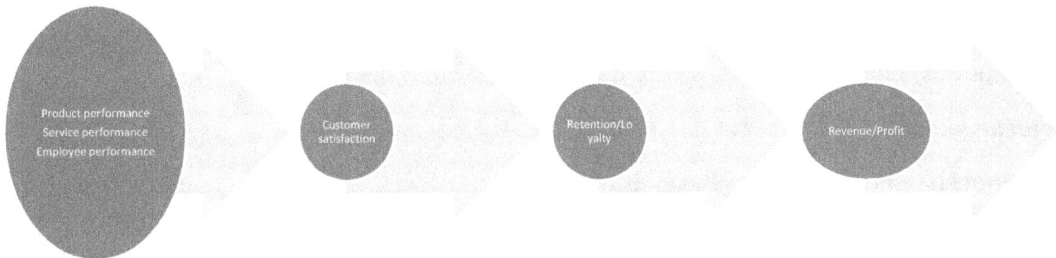

The Customer Profit Chain is a concept that shows the link between customer satisfaction, loyalty, and a company's profitability. It illustrates how happy customers contribute to a business's success. Happy customers are satisfied with the products or services they receive. Satisfaction is the feeling of contentment and happiness that customers experience when their expectations are met or exceeded. Satisfied customers are more likely to continue doing business with a company and recommend it to others. Satisfied customers are more likely to stick with a brand and make repeat purchases. Loyalty leads to customer retention, where customers continue to choose a particular brand over time. Loyalty is the customer's commitment to consistently choose a particular brand or company over its competitors. Retention refers to the ability of a business to keep its customers over an extended period. Loyal customers not only continue to make purchases but also contribute to a company's stability and long-term success.

Let's take an example of a coffee Shop Chain which ensures quality coffee, friendly service, and a cozy atmosphere. Satisfied customers keep coming back to the same coffee shop for their daily brew. Over time, these loyal customers become regulars, contributing to the coffee shop's steady stream of business.

Importance of the Chain:

1. Satisfied and loyal customers are more likely to make repeat purchases.
2. Happy customers become brand advocates, recommending the business to friends and family.
3. Acquiring new customers is often more expensive than retaining existing ones.

Link between satisfaction and retention:

Dissatisfaction's Impact on Retention:

Retention is more significantly influenced by dissatisfaction than satisfaction. Successfully retaining a customer generally requires a foundation of satisfaction. For example, a telecom company experiencing frequent service outages might find that dissatisfied customers are more likely to switch to a competitor.

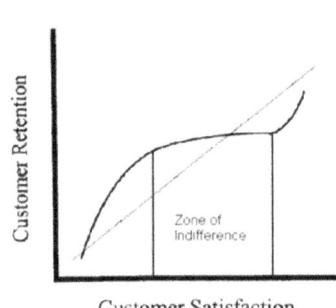

No Guarantee with High Satisfaction:

Despite high satisfaction levels, retention is not assured. Intense competition offering similar products can still lure customers away. For example, a customer might be highly satisfied with their current smartphone, but a new model with innovative features from a competitor might still attract them.

Dissatisfaction and Alternatives:

Dissatisfied customers are more open to exploring alternatives. Competing products become more appealing when dissatisfaction sets in. for example, a diner dissatisfied with a restaurant's service might be more inclined to try out a new restaurant in the vicinity.

Non-linear Impact:

The relationship is non-linear, meaning the impact of satisfaction on retention is more pronounced at the extremes. Regular customers, for instance, may enjoy additional benefits, enhancing their loyalty. For example, a frequent flyer program offering exclusive perks for loyal customers incentivizes them to stick with a particular airline.

Zone of Indifference:

The middle of the satisfaction-retention curve is the "zone of indifference." Small changes in price or benefits in this zone have minimal impact on customer behavior. For example, a slight increase in the cost of a streaming service in the "zone of indifference" might not lead to a significant loss of subscribers.

Influencing Factors:

The shape of the curve and the positions of the elbows are influenced by factors like competition aggressiveness, switching costs, and perceived risk. For example, in a crowded market, where competitors offer similar benefits, switching costs become a crucial factor in shaping the satisfaction-retention curve.

Connection between Customer Satisfaction and Profit:

Direct Link to Profits: Increasing customer satisfaction directly correlates with higher profits. A positive customer experience contributes to enhanced satisfaction, fostering customer loyalty and repeated business. For example, a software company providing excellent customer support may see increased sales as satisfied customers recommend their products to others.

Correlation with Return on Assets:

There is a consistent positive correlation between customer satisfaction and return on assets. A satisfied customer base contributes to the financial health of the company. For example, a retail store with high customer satisfaction scores may experience increased foot traffic and sales, positively impacting its return on assets.

Cost of Satisfaction Improvement:

Improving customer satisfaction comes with a cost. However, going beyond a certain level of satisfaction may not yield proportional returns. For example, a luxury car manufacturer investing in premium customer service may reach a point where further enhancements provide diminishing returns.

Diminishing Marginal Gains:

As satisfaction improves, the marginal gains decrease, while the expenses to achieve additional satisfaction growth increase. For example, a hotel chain investing in room upgrades and personalized services may find that each incremental improvement in satisfaction requires a higher financial investment.

Optimum Satisfaction Level:

There is an optimum satisfaction level for any firm, beyond which further efforts to increase satisfaction may not justify the associated costs. For example, a technology company may identify a satisfaction level where customer loyalty is high, and additional investments in satisfaction improvement may not significantly impact profitability.

Strategies for Customer Profit Chain:

1. Ensure that your offerings meet or exceed customer expectations.
2. Provide excellent customer support to address concerns and build trust.
3. Offer rewards to encourage repeat business and loyalty.

Example: (Apple)

Satisfaction:

Apple focuses on product design, user experience, and innovation.

Loyalty:

Satisfied customers often stick with Apple, buying iPhones, iPads, and other Apple products.

Retention:

Apple's customer base remains loyal, contributing to its consistent success in the tech market.

CRM STRATEGY (Nov., 2022; Nov., 2018)

CRM, which stands for Customer Relationship Management, is a strategy that businesses use to manage and analyze customer interactions throughout the customer lifecycle. The

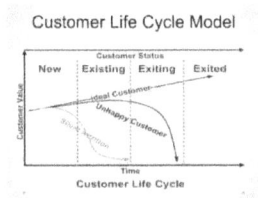

Customer Lifecycle, also known as the Customer Journey, refers to the stages that a customer goes through from the initial awareness of a product or service to the eventual purchase, and beyond. Understanding the customer lifecycle is crucial for businesses as it helps in tailoring marketing, sales, and customer service strategies to meet the specific needs and expectations of customers at each stage. The goal of CRM is to improve customer retention, drive sales growth, and enhance overall customer satisfaction. A CRM strategy involves using technology to organize, automate, and synchronize sales, marketing, customer service, and technical support. Components of a CRM strategy includes:

Customer Data Management:

Collecting and storing relevant customer information, such as contact details, purchase history, and preferences, in a centralized database.

Sales Automation:

Streamlining sales processes and automating repetitive tasks to improve efficiency, such as lead management, opportunity tracking, and sales forecasting.

Marketing Automation:

Using technology to automate marketing tasks, such as email campaigns, social media posting, and targeted advertising, to better engage and nurture leads.

Customer Service and Support:

Implementing tools and processes to provide excellent customer service, resolve issues promptly, and maintain positive customer relationships.

Analytics and Reporting:

Utilizing data analytics to gain insights into customer behavior, preferences, and trends, helping businesses make informed decisions and refine their strategies.

Integration:

Ensuring seamless integration between different departments and systems within the organization to have a unified view of customer interactions.

Objectives of a CRM (Customer Relationship Management) strategy

1. Retain existing customers and build long-term relationships. For example, implement loyalty programs, personalized discounts, and exclusive offers for repeat customers.
2. Attract and acquire new customers. For example, use CRM data to identify leads and run targeted marketing campaigns, such as offering promotions to first-time buyers.
3. Improve overall customer satisfaction. For example, ensure quick response times to customer inquiries, personalized customer service interactions, and efficient issue resolution.
4. Streamline and optimize sales processes. For example, implement CRM automation for lead scoring, automated follow-up emails, and sales pipeline management to reduce manual tasks and increase efficiency.
5. Implement targeted and personalized marketing strategies. For example, segment customers based on their preferences and purchase history to send personalized email campaigns or recommend products tailored to their interests.
6. Make informed decisions based on customer data. For example, analyze CRM data to identify high-performing products, customer demographics, and market trends, guiding decisions on inventory management and marketing strategies.
7. Increase revenue through cross-selling and upselling opportunities. For example, recommend complementary products or premium versions based on a customer's purchase history and preferences.
8. Enhance communication with customers across channels. For example, use CRM to centralize communication history, allowing customer support representatives to provide personalized assistance and respond consistently across various channels.
9. Boost productivity and collaboration among teams. For example, enable sales and customer service teams to access centralized customer data, track interactions, and collaborate on strategies to enhance customer satisfaction.
10. Quickly adapt to evolving customer preferences and market trends. For example, monitor CRM analytics to identify shifts in customer behavior, enabling businesses to modify product offerings or marketing approaches to meet changing needs.

The CRM (Customer Relationship Management) Strategy Cycle: (Nov., 2019; April, 2019)

The CRM strategy cycle encompasses customer acquisition, customer retention, and the win-back stage.

Customer Relationship Management

Customer Acquisition:

Attract and acquire new customers to expand the customer base. Identify target audience and segments and run targeted marketing campaigns to reach potential customers. Further, utilize lead generation strategies to capture prospective customer information. For example, a new e-commerce startup launches a social media advertising campaign targeting users interested in similar products. The campaign offers a special discount for first-time customers, encouraging them to make their first purchase.

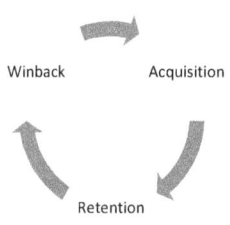

Customer Retention:

Retain existing customers by building strong relationships and providing value. Implement loyalty programs and rewards for repeat purchases and provide personalized customer service and support. Also use CRM data for targeted marketing to existing customers. For example, a subscription-based streaming service offers exclusive content and personalized recommendations based on users' viewing history. They also provide loyalty rewards such as early access to new releases for long-term subscribers.

Win-Back Stage:

Re-engage with inactive or former customers to bring them back into the customer base. Analyze customer behavior and reasons for disengagement and design targeted win-back campaigns. Also offer incentives or promotions to encourage reactivation. For example, a retail brand identifies customers who haven't made a purchase in the last six months. They send personalized emails with a special discount or a limited-time offer to entice these customers to return and make a purchase.

Steps in successful implementation of CRM Strategy Cycle:

Customer Data Analysis:

Continuously analyze customer data to understand behavior and preferences. Regularly update customer profiles with new data. Use analytics tools to identify trends and patterns. Tailor marketing and communication strategies based on data insights. For example, an online marketplace uses data analytics to identify popular product categories among different customer segments. They then customize their homepage and email campaigns to highlight these preferred products for each segment.

Personalized Communication:

Engage customers with personalized communication across various channels. Implement automated communication workflows. Send personalized messages based on customer preferences. Utilize CRM tools for targeted email campaigns. For example, an airline sends personalized travel itineraries, exclusive offers, and seat upgrade options to frequent flyers based on their travel history and preferences.

Feedback Collection and Improvement:

Gather customer feedback to identify areas for improvement and enhance the overall customer experience. Conduct surveys and gather feedback through various channels. Analyze feedback to identify strengths and weaknesses. Implement changes based on customer suggestions. For example, a software company collects feedback from users through in-app surveys and social media. They use this feedback to prioritize features for the next software update, addressing users' needs and concerns.

Complexities of CRM Strategy: (Nov., 2019)

1. Incomplete or inaccurate data can lead to flawed analytics, affecting decision-making and customer interactions.
2. Scalability challenges may arise as the organization expands, requiring system upgrades and adjustments to handle larger datasets.
3. Resistance to change, lack of training, or perceived complexity can hinder user adoption, impacting the overall success of the CRM strategy.
4. Overly customized systems may become rigid and challenging to adapt, while highly flexible systems might lack the specificity needed for certain business processes.
5. With increasing data breaches and privacy concerns, organizations need to implement robust security measures to protect sensitive customer information.
6. Customer expectations are dynamic, and a CRM strategy must adapt to changing customer behaviors, technologies, and market trends to remain effective.

PLANNING OF CRM (April, 2023; Nov., 2019; April, 2019; Nov., 2018)

Following steps are included in planning of CRM.

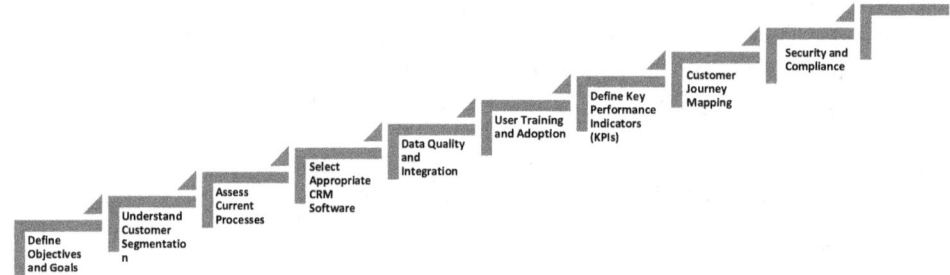

Define Objectives and Goals:

Clearly articulate the business objectives and goals that the CRM strategy aims to achieve. For example, a telecommunications company might set a goal to reduce customer churn by 15% within the next six months.

Understand Customer Segmentation:

Identify and understand the different segments of your customer base. For example, an e-commerce company segments its customers into categories such as "first-time buyers," "loyal customers," and "discount seekers" based on their purchasing behavior.

Assess Current Processes:

Evaluate existing sales, marketing, and customer service processes. For example, a software development company conducts an analysis of its current lead management process to identify bottlenecks and areas for improvement.

Select Appropriate CRM Software:

Choose CRM software that aligns with business needs and objectives. For example, an IT consulting firm selects a CRM platform that integrates seamlessly with its project management tools and provides robust reporting features.

Data Quality and Integration:

Ensure the accuracy and integration of customer data. For example, a healthcare organization plans for data cleansing activities before migrating patient records to the new CRM system to ensure data accuracy and consistency.

User Training and Adoption:

Plan for comprehensive user training to encourage CRM system adoption. For example, a retail business conducts workshops to train its sales staff on using the new CRM system for customer interactions, order processing, and inventory management.

Define Key Performance Indicators (KPIs):

Establish measurable KPIs to track the success of the CRM strategy. For example, a financial institution defines KPIs such as average customer response time, customer satisfaction scores, and lead conversion rates to measure the impact of its CRM efforts.

Customer Journey Mapping:

Map out the customer journey to understand touchpoints and interactions. For example, an airline identifies key touchpoints in the customer journey, from booking a flight online to post-trip feedback, to enhance the overall travel experience.

Security and Compliance:

Develop robust security measures and ensure compliance with data protection regulations. For example, a legal services firm implements encryption and access controls to protect client data and ensures compliance with privacy regulations like GDPR.

BUSINESS TO BUSINESS (B2B) CRM: (April, 2019)

B2B CRM (Business-to-Business Customer Relationship Management) involves strategies and tools designed specifically for managing relationships with other businesses. B2B CRM focuses on managing and optimizing interactions and relationships between businesses, typically involving longer sales cycles and more complex decision-making processes. B2B sales cycles are usually more intricate, requiring CRM systems that allow for flexible and customizable sales processes. For example, a B2B company utilizes Salesforce to manage its sales processes.

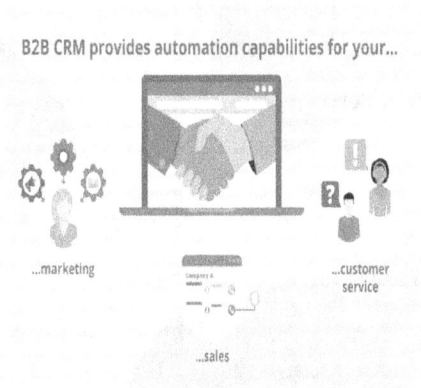

Salesforce allows the company to create detailed customer profiles, track communications, and forecast sales based on historical data. It also facilitates collaboration among sales teams and integrates with marketing tools for lead generation. B2B CRM systems prioritize data security due to the sensitive nature of business information. B2B CRM systems also offers mobile accessibility, enabling sales teams to access critical information while on the go.

PRICEWATERHOUSE COOPERS (PWC) came out with the concept of **Market Intelligence Enterprise** to anticipate the future needs of key customers and fulfilling them before they move to the competitor.

Introduction to Market Intelligence: Market Intelligence refers to the process of gathering, analyzing, and interpreting information about a company's market, competitors, customers, and industry trends. It helps businesses make informed decisions, identify opportunities, and stay ahead in a competitive landscape. The steps involved in MIE are as under:

Step 1: Define Objectives

Determine the purpose of developing a Market Intelligence enterprise. Are you looking to understand customer preferences, track competitors, or identify new market trends?

Step 2: Identify Information Needs

Recognize the type of information required to achieve the set objectives. This can include customer demographics, competitor strategies, market size, and growth potential.

Step 3: Collect Data

Utilize various sources to gather data. Examples include surveys, interviews, online research, government publications, industry reports, and social media platforms. For example, conduct surveys and interviews to understand customer preferences and buying behavior. Analyze online reviews and comments to gather insights about your competitors.

Step 4: Organize and Analyze Data

Organize the collected data into a structured format to facilitate analysis. Use tools like spreadsheets or specialized software for data analysis. For example, create a database of competitor product features, pricing, and marketing strategies for easy comparison.

Step 5: Interpret Findings

Analyze the data to derive meaningful insights. Identify patterns, trends, strengths, weaknesses, opportunities, and threats. For example, identify emerging market trends and align your product development strategy accordingly.

Step 6: Prepare Reports

Present the findings in a clear and concise manner. Use graphs, charts, and visual aids to enhance understanding. For example, create a market intelligence report highlighting the market potential for a new product launch, supported by data and analysis.

Step 7: Implement Findings

Translate the insights into actionable strategies. Share the findings with relevant teams and incorporate them into business plans. For example, based on the intelligence gathered, adjust marketing campaigns or pricing strategies to better target your audience.

Step 8: Monitor and Update

Market dynamics change continuously, so regularly update your intelligence enterprise. Monitor key metrics and revise strategies accordingly. For example, continuously track competitor activities and customer feedback to stay informed and adaptable.

MARKET INFORMATION VS MARKET INTELLIGENCE

MARKET INFORMATION
Collecting information is just the first step in the marketing-intelligence process.

Information is created by numbers and some statistics about your customers, products, and competitors.

This information needs to be analyzed in order to gain valuable insights from it.

VS

MARKET INTELLIGENCE
Information becomes intelligence when it's analyzed.

Analzing information involves activities such as using appropriate software systems, dashboards, data visualization tools, graphs and etc.

this way, companies can use marketing intelligence to take business decisions.

CROSS BORDER B2B RELATIONSHIP WITH INTERMEDIARIES

Cross-border B2B relationships with intermediaries involve business-to-business transactions that span international borders and are facilitated by intermediaries or third-party entities. Intermediaries play a crucial role in facilitating and enhancing these relationships by bridging gaps, managing complexities, and providing value-added services. Before entering into a cross-border relationship with an intermediary, conduct thorough due diligence. Understand and comply with local laws and regulations governing B2B relationships, including contracts, intellectual property, and dispute resolution mechanisms. Clear and effective communication is essential. Establish regular communication channels, provide training as needed, and maintain a collaborative relationship. Be flexible and adaptable to changes in the market, regulatory environment, and customer preferences. Regularly assess the performance of your intermediary relationships and adjust as necessary.

The features of cross-border B2B relationship with intermediaries are as under:

Agents and Distributors:

These entities represent your company in the foreign market. Agents typically earn commissions for sales, while distributors purchase and resell your products.

Trading Companies:

These companies buy products from your business and sell them in international markets. They can provide market access and handle logistics.

Advantages:

Local Expertise:

Intermediaries often have a deep understanding of local markets, regulations, and business practices, which can be invaluable for a foreign company.

Risk Mitigation:

Intermediaries can help mitigate risks associated with currency fluctuations, regulatory compliance, and cultural differences.

Efficiency:

They can streamline logistics, distribution, and sales processes, making it more efficient for your business to operate in a foreign market.

Challenges:

1. Relying on intermediaries means relinquishing some degree of control over the sales and distribution process.
2. Differences in language and culture may lead to misunderstandings, affecting the success of the partnership.
3. Over-reliance on a single intermediary can pose risks if their business experiences issues.

SALES AND CRM (April, 2019)

CRM and sales are closely interconnected, with CRM serving as a comprehensive strategy and technology to manage customer relationships, and sales being a crucial component of customer interactions. CRM systems assist in capturing, tracking, and nurturing leads through the sales funnel. Sales teams use CRM to manage and track opportunities, ensuring a systematic approach to deal progression. For example, HubSpot provides a CRM system that seamlessly integrates with its Sales Hub, allowing businesses to manage leads, automate tasks, and gain insights into sales performance.

SALESFORCE AUTOMATION: (April, 2023; April, 2019)

Salesforce Automation (SFA) refers to the use of software tools and technologies to streamline and automate the sales process within an organization. The primary goal of Salesforce Automation is to enhance the efficiency and effectiveness of sales teams by automating repetitive tasks, managing customer interactions, and providing insights to improve decision-making.

The various functions of Salesforce Automation is shown as under:

Contact and Lead Management:

SFA systems help in organizing and tracking customer information, including leads and contacts. For example, a salesperson can use the platform to input and manage leads acquired from marketing campaigns.

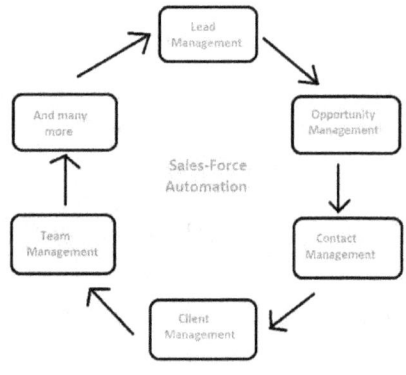

Opportunity Management:

Salesforce Automation allows sales teams to manage and track sales opportunities through various stages of the sales pipeline. For example, a sales representative can update the status of an opportunity, add relevant details, and track the probability of closing a deal.

Task and Activity Management:

Users can schedule and manage tasks and activities, ensuring that sales representatives stay organized and follow up on leads and opportunities. For example, a salesperson can set reminders for follow-up calls, meetings, or sending out proposals.

Quoting and Proposal Generation:

SFA tools often include features for creating and managing quotes and proposals. This can streamline the process of generating customized quotes for potential customers.

Forecasting:

Salesforce Automation enables sales teams to forecast future sales based on historical data and current opportunities. This helps organizations make informed decisions about resource allocation and revenue projections.

Workflow Automation:

SFA systems often include workflow automation capabilities, allowing organizations to automate routine tasks and processes. For instance, when a lead reaches a certain stage in the sales pipeline, an automated email can be triggered to follow up with the prospect.

Integration with Other Systems:

SFA platforms can integrate with other business systems, such as marketing automation, customer relationship management (CRM), and ERP systems. This ensures seamless data flow and a holistic view of customer interactions.

Example of Sales Force Automation:

Imagine a salesperson, Sarah, working for a furniture company. The role of SFA is as under:

Contact Management: SFA stores all customer details, like names, phone numbers, and addresses in one place. When Sarah meets a new customer, she adds their information to the software

Lead Management: Sarah receives inquiries from potential customers through the company's website. SFA automatically captures these leads and reminds Sarah to follow u with them.

Opportunity Management: Sarah identifies a potential sale with a hotel that needs new furniture. She creates an opportunity in the SFA system, tracks the progress, and updates notes after every interaction.

Sales Forecasting: The software analyses past sales data and trends. Based on this, Sarah's manager can predict how much furniture the team is likely to sell in the upcoming months. Order Processing: Once Sarah finalizes a deal with hotel, she enters the order details into the SFA system. This information is sent to the production team, ensuring a smooth order fulfilment process.

Reporting and Analytics: At the end of the month, Sarah's manager generates a report from the SFA system. It shows how many deals Sarah closed, the revenue generated, and which products were popular among customers.

Benefits of Sales Force Automation:

Time-Saving: SFA reduces manual work, allowing Sarah to spend more time with customers.

Better Customer Service: Sarah has all customer information at her fingertips, making easy to provide personalized service.

Improved Productivity: With SFA handling routine tasks, Sarah can focus on selling an meeting her targets.

Accurate Sales Forecasting: The software helps in predicting future sales, helping the comp plan better.

Consistency in Sales Process: SFA ensures that all salespeople follow the same steps, leading to fewer mistakes.

ACTIVITY MANAGEMENT:

Activity management involves planning, organizing, and controlling tasks and processes to achieve specific goals or objectives efficiently. It is a systematic approach to ensure that activities are carried out in a coordinated and effective manner. This concept is often applied in various fields, including business, project management, and personal productivity.

Let's take a business example to illustrate activity management:

Suppose you are a project manager responsible for organizing a software development project. Activity management in this context would involve breaking down the project into smaller tasks, assigning responsibilities to team members, setting timelines, and monitoring progress.

Planning: Identify the different tasks required for software development, such as coding, testing, and documentation. Estimate the time and resources needed for each task.

Organizing: Assign specific tasks to individual team members based on their skills and expertise. Create a schedule that outlines when each task should be completed.

Controlling: Monitor the progress of the project regularly. If a task is behind schedule or faces unexpected challenges, take corrective actions, such as reallocating resources or adjusting timelines.

SALES TERRITORY MANAGEMENT:

Sales territory management is the process of dividing a market into geographic areas to optimize the allocation of sales resources and enhance overall sales performance. The goal is to strategically assign sales representatives to specific territories, ensuring that they can effectively reach and serve their target customers. This practice helps in maximizing efficiency, improving customer relationships, and ultimately driving sales growth.

An example of sales territory management:

Imagine you work for a technology company that sells software and hardware solutions. The company operates in a large geographic area and has identified different regions where it wants to establish a strong market presence.

Step 1: The first step in sales territory management is to define the territories. In this case, the company might divide the market into regions, such as North, South, East, and West. Each region represents a sales territory.

Step 2: After that, the company assesses its sales team and resources. Based on the size of the market and potential business opportunities, it decides how many sales representatives to assign to each territory. For example, the North region might have a larger sales team due to its higher market potential.

Step 3: Within each territory, the company identifies different customer segments. For instance, it might categorize customers based on industry, company size, or specific needs. This segmentation helps sales representatives tailor their approaches to different types of customers.

Step 4: The company sets sales targets and goals for each territory. These goals are based on factors such as market potential, historical performance, and overall business strategy. Sales representatives in each territory are then responsible for achieving these targets.

Step 5: Regular monitoring of sales performance in each territory is essential. If a particular region is consistently underperforming or if there are changes in the market dynamics, the company may adjust territory boundaries, reallocate resources, or implement new strategies to address challenges.

CONTACT MANAGEMENT: (Nov., 2022)

Contact management involves organizing and managing an organization's interactions with its contacts, which can include customers, clients, suppliers, or any other individuals or entities with whom the organization engages. The goal is to maintain accurate and up-to-date information about these contacts, facilitate communication, and enhance relationships. This is commonly done through contact management software.

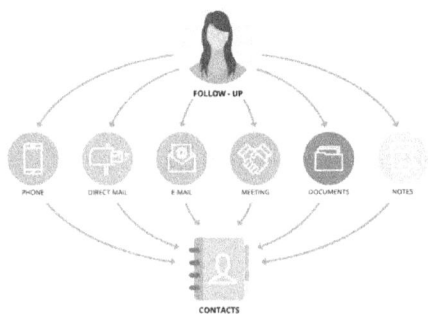

For example, you run a small consulting business, and you have various clients, partners, and suppliers to manage. In this context, contact management would involve using software to organize and maintain information about these contacts. You input contact details such as names, phone numbers, email addresses, and other relevant information into the contact management system. This system allows you to create a comprehensive database of all your business contacts. After this, contacts are categorized based on different criteria, such as clients, suppliers, leads, etc. This categorization helps in quickly identifying and retrieving relevant information when needed. Further, the contact management software tracks all interactions with each contact. This includes emails, phone calls, meetings, and any other communication. This history provides a valuable reference for understanding the context of your relationship with each contact. Tasks and reminders can be set related to specific contacts. For instance, you might set a reminder to follow up with a client about an ongoing project or to send a thank-you email to a supplier after completing a successful transaction.

Many contact management systems integrate with other tools, such as email clients or customer relationship management (CRM) software. This ensures that information is synchronized across different platforms and enhances overall efficiency.

LEAD MANAGEMENT:

Customer Relationship Management

Lead management is the process of capturing, tracking, and nurturing potential customers or leads throughout their journey from initial contact to conversion. The goal is to systematically manage leads to increase the likelihood of turning them into customers. This involves various activities, including lead generation, qualification, distribution, and follow-up.

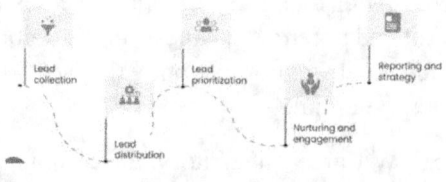

Importance of Lead Management:

Maximizing Lead Conversion: An effective lead management system ensures that no potential sales opportunity falls through the cracks. It increases the chances of converting leads into paying customers.

Streamlining Sales Processes: Lead management helps sales teams prioritize leads and focus on those with higher potential, making their efforts more efficient and productive.

Personalized Engagement: Nurturing leads through personalized communication and targeted marketing campaigns builds trust and strengthens the relationship with potential customers.

Data-Driven Insights: Lead management systems provide valuable data and insights into lead behaviour, helping businesses make data-driven decisions and optimize their sales and marketing strategies.

For example, the company uses various online channels, such as its website, social media platforms, and email campaigns, to generate leads. Visitors who express interest in products by signing up for newsletters, downloading product guides, or entering their contact information are considered leads. The retailer employs lead capture mechanisms on its website, such as contact forms or pop-ups, to collect information from potential customers. This information includes names, email addresses, and perhaps preferences related to product categories. Not all leads are equal in terms of their readiness to make a purchase. The retailer uses lead qualification criteria to assess the level of interest and potential of each lead. For example, a lead who has browsed specific product categories or has provided detailed information might be considered a higher-priority lead. Once leads are captured and qualified, they are distributed among sales representatives or teams. This distribution can be based on factors like geographic location, product specialization, or sales capacity. For instance, leads from a specific region might be assigned to a local sales representative. Sales representatives follow up with the assigned leads to provide additional information, answer questions, and guide them through the purchase process. Automated email campaigns and personalized content may be used to nurture leads over time, keeping the brand top of mind. The company uses tracking tools and analytics to monitor the entire lead management process. This includes tracking the performance of different marketing channels, analyzing conversion rates at each stage, and identifying areas for improvement.

The ultimate goal of lead management is to convert leads into customers. Through effective lead nurturing, personalized communication, and timely follow-up, the online retailer increases the likelihood that a lead will make a purchase.

CONFIGURATION MANAGEMENT:

Configuration management is a discipline that involves the systematic management of an organization's configurations, including its hardware, software, documentation, and other components. The goal is to establish and maintain the consistency and integrity of the system's performance, functionality, and attributes throughout its life cycle. Configuration management is crucial in industries such as IT, engineering, and manufacturing where complex systems are developed and maintained.

Importance of Configuration Management:

Version Control: Configuration Management enables version control, ensuring that project stakeholders work with the same up-to-date information, reducing the risk of and miscommunication.

Quality Assurance: By maintaining strict control over configurations, Configuration Management ensures that project deliverables meet quality standards and are free from defects.

Risk Management: Identifying and managing configuration changes helps mitigate potential risks, reducing the chances of project delays and cost overruns.

Traceability: Configuration Management provides a clear audit trail of all changes, make it easier to trace the history of a project's components and quickly identify the source of issues that may arise.

For example, imagine a software development company that creates and maintains a complex web application. Configuration management in this context involves overseeing the various elements that make up the software, including code, databases, third-party libraries, and server configurations. One of the fundamental aspects of configuration management is version control. The software development team uses a version control system (e.g., Git) to manage changes to the source code. Each change made by a developer is tracked, and different versions of the codebase are maintained.

Configuration management includes managing the build and deployment processes. The configuration manager ensures that the correct versions of source code, libraries, and configurations are used to create a build. This ensures consistency between the development, testing, and production environments.

KNOWLEDGE MANAGEMENT: (Nov., 2019; Nov., 2018)

Knowledge management (KM) is the process of capturing, organizing, storing, and sharing an organization's collective knowledge to facilitate learning, decision-making, and innovation. It involves creating an environment where knowledge is systematically gathered, managed, and made accessible to individuals within the organization. Knowledge management aims to improve efficiency, enhance collaboration, and foster innovation by leveraging the expertise and insights of individuals.

Importance of Knowledge Management:

Knowledge Retention and Continuity: In an era of workforce mobility, Knowledge Management ensures that critical knowledge doesn't leave with employees who may re or move on, ensuring continuity and reducing the impact of knowledge loss.

Informed Decision-Making: Knowledge Management provides decision-makers with accurate and relevant information, allowing thére to make informed choices that align w the organization's objectives.

Improved Problem-Solving: By sharing best practices and past experiences, Knowledge Management facilitates more effective problem-solving and faster resolution of challenge Innovation and Learning: Access to a wealth of knowledge encourages continuous learning and fosters a culture of innovation, driving business growth and adaptability

Components of Knowledge Management:

Knowledge Capture: Identifying and capturing knowledge from various sources, such experts, documents, databases, and organizational processes.

Knowledge Organization: Classifying and organizing knowledge in a structured manner using taxonomies, categories, and metadata for easy retrieval.

Knowledge Storage: Storing knowledge in centralized repositories or knowledge bases accessible to relevant employees.

Knowledge Sharing: Facilitating collaboration and sharing of knowledge among employee

through forums, intranets, and knowledge-sharing platforms.

Knowledge Transfer: Ensuring knowledge transfer from experienced employees to new team members through mentorship and training programs

Benefits of Knowledge Management:

Enhanced Productivity: Easy access to knowledge streamlines work processes, reducing duplication of efforts and enhancing overall productivity.

Faster Problem Resolution: Employees can quickly find solutions to challenges by accessing previous solutions and best practices.

Effective Decision-Making: Knowledge-based decisions are more informed, reducing ris and increasing the likelihood of success.

Cultivating a Learning Culture: Knowledge Management promotes continuous learning and knowledge-sharing, leading to a more adaptive and innovative organizational culture

Let's explore knowledge management with an example:

Imagine a consulting firm that specializes in providing strategic business solutions to its clients. Knowledge management is crucial for the firm to leverage the collective expertise of its consultants and deliver high-quality services. Consultants engage in various projects, and each project generates valuable insights, solutions, and lessons learned. Knowledge management involves capturing this tacit and explicit knowledge. For instance, after completing a successful project, consultants might document the challenges faced, the strategies employed, and the outcomes achieved. The collected knowledge is organized in a structured manner. This could involve categorizing information based on industries, project types, or specific expertise areas. For example, the firm might create a knowledge repository that contains case studies, best practices, and templates for different business sectors. A central knowledge repository, often facilitated by knowledge management software, is established to store and manage the documented knowledge. This repository can include documents, presentations, videos, and any other format that effectively captures and communicates knowledge. Consultants within the firm have access to the knowledge repository. They can retrieve relevant information when needed, whether it's to prepare for a client meeting, learn from past experiences, or incorporate best practices into new projects. This access helps in avoiding the reinvention of the wheel and promotes consistent and high-quality service delivery.

Knowledge management fosters collaboration among consultants. For example, if a consultant is facing a challenging problem on a project, they can use the knowledge repository to identify colleagues with expertise in that area. They can then reach out for advice or collaborate on finding a solution, promoting a culture of shared learning.

Knowledge management is not a static process. It involves continuous improvement and updating of the knowledge repository. For instance, after completing a project, consultants may participate in a debriefing session to discuss what worked well, what could be improved, and update the knowledge repository accordingly.

CRM IMPLEMENTATION (April, 2023; Nov., 2019; April, 2019; Nov., 2018)

Customer Relationship Management (CRM) implementation is the process of adopting and integrating a CRM system into an organization to effectively manage and enhance relationships with customers. Successful CRM implementation involves careful planning, customization, and training to ensure that the CRM system aligns with the organization's goals and processes. Below are the steps involved in CRM implementation, explained in detail with examples:

Objectives and Scope:

Clearly define the goals and objectives of implementing CRM. This could include improving customer satisfaction, increasing sales, or streamlining communication. For example, an e-commerce company may aim to improve customer retention and satisfaction by implementing a CRM system to personalize customer interactions and offer targeted promotions.

Assemble a Project Team:

Form a dedicated project team with representatives from different departments, including sales, marketing, customer service, and IT. For example, the project team could consist of a sales manager, marketing specialist, customer service representative, and IT professionals.

Select a CRM System:

Choose a CRM system that aligns with the organization's needs and goals. Consider factors such as features, scalability, and integration capabilities. For example, a medium-sized manufacturing company may choose a CRM system that integrates with its existing ERP (Enterprise Resource Planning) system to streamline processes.

Customize the CRM System:

Tailor the CRM system to match the organization's workflows and business processes. This may involve configuring fields, workflows, and user interfaces. For example, customizing the CRM system to automate lead qualification processes, ensuring that leads are routed to the appropriate sales representatives based on predefined criteria.

Data Migration:

Transfer existing customer data from legacy systems or spreadsheets to the new CRM system. Ensure data accuracy and consistency during the migration. For example, importing customer contact details, purchase history, and support ticket information from the old system to the new CRM database.

Integration with Other Systems:

Integrate the CRM system with other enterprise systems, such as ERP or marketing automation tools, to create a unified data environment. For example, integrating the CRM system with the company's email marketing platform to synchronize customer communication data and improve marketing campaign targeting.

User Training:

Train users on how to effectively use the CRM system. This includes understanding data entry, reporting, and utilizing advanced features. For example, conducting workshops and providing online training modules to teach sales representatives how to use the CRM system to track leads, manage opportunities, and generate reports.

Testing:

Conduct thorough testing to identify and address any issues or bugs in the system before full deployment. For example, testing the CRM system's functionality, data accuracy, and user interfaces in a controlled environment to ensure that it meets the organization's requirements.

Rollout and Adoption:

Gradually implement the CRM system across the organization, ensuring that users adopt and adapt to the new technology. For example, rolling out the CRM system department by department, starting with the sales team, and progressively extending its use to other areas like marketing and customer service.

Monitor and Optimize:

Continuously monitor the CRM system's performance, gather user feedback, and optimize its effectiveness. For example, regularly reviewing key performance indicators (KPIs) such as customer satisfaction, sales revenue, and lead conversion rates to identify areas for improvement and refinement.

CRM EVALUATION

CRM (Customer Relationship Management) evaluation is the process of assessing and selecting a CRM system that aligns with an organization's business needs and objectives. The steps involved in CRM evaluation:

Customer Relationship Management

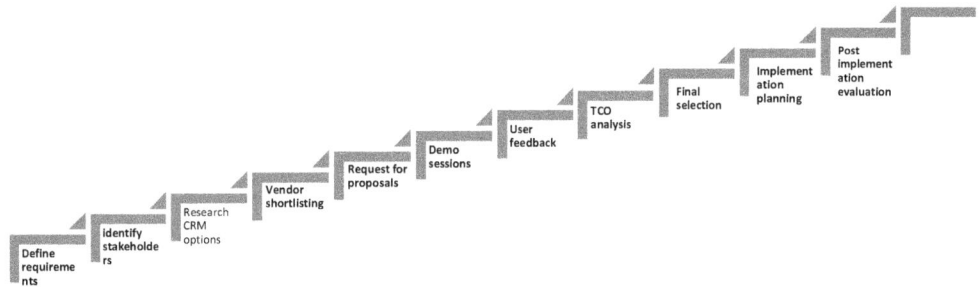

Define Requirements:

Clearly outline the specific needs and requirements of your organization. This involves understanding your business processes, customer interactions, and the data you need to manage. For example, if your organization heavily relies on lead generation, you might need a CRM that has robust lead management features.

Identify Stakeholders:

Identify the key stakeholders and users who will be involved in the CRM system. Their input is crucial to understanding user needs and expectations. For example, sales representatives, marketing teams, and customer support staff are key stakeholders who may have different requirements.

Research CRM Options:

Description: Conduct thorough research on available CRM solutions in the market. Consider factors such as features, scalability, integration capabilities, and user reviews. For example, Salesforce, HubSpot, and Zoho CRM are popular CRM solutions with various features and pricing structures.

Vendor Shortlisting:

Shortlist CRM vendors based on how well their solutions align with your requirements. Consider factors like budget, user-friendliness, and the vendor's reputation. For example, after research, you may shortlist Salesforce and HubSpot as potential CRM vendors.

Request for Proposals (RFPs):

Create a Request for Proposal document and send it to the shortlisted vendors. This document outlines your specific requirements and asks vendors to provide details on how their CRM meets these needs. For example, your RFP may include questions about customization options, data security, and pricing structures.

Demo Sessions:

Arrange demo sessions with the shortlisted vendors to see their CRM systems in action. This helps you assess the usability and functionality of the CRM. For example, during a demo, you might explore how the CRM handles lead tracking and management.

User Feedback:

Collect feedback from potential users who participated in the demo sessions. This helps in understanding how well the CRM meets their day-to-day operational needs. For example, sales representatives might provide feedback on the ease of use and effectiveness in managing customer interactions.

Total Cost of Ownership (TCO) Analysis:

Evaluate the total cost of ownership, including licensing fees, implementation costs, and ongoing maintenance. This step ensures that the chosen CRM fits within your budget. For example, consider the costs associated with user training, customization, and any additional modules you may need.

Final Selection:

Based on the evaluation, select the CRM system that best meets your organization's requirements, considering user feedback, costs, and overall fit. For example, choose Salesforce as your CRM solution due to its comprehensive features, positive user feedback, and scalability.

Implementation Planning:

Develop a detailed plan for CRM implementation. This includes data migration, user training, and integration with existing systems. For example, plan a phased implementation approach, starting with a pilot group to minimize disruption.

Post-Implementation Evaluation:

After implementation, assess the performance of the CRM system. Gather feedback from users and make any necessary adjustments. For example, monitor how well the CRM system improves customer interactions and sales processes over time.

SERVICE QUALITY IN ACHIEVING CUSTOMER SATISFACTION:

Service quality refers to the level of excellence or adequacy of services provided by a business to meet the expectations and needs of its customers. Achieving customer satisfaction is closely linked to delivering high service quality. Several dimensions contribute to service quality, and meeting or exceeding customer expectations in these areas can enhance overall satisfaction. These dimensions are discussed as under:

Reliability:

The ability of a service provider to consistently deliver accurate and dependable services. For example, an online banking platform that ensures transactions are processed accurately and reliably without errors, ensuring customers can trust the system for their financial activities.

Responsiveness:

The willingness and ability of a service provider to help customers and provide prompt service. For example, a customer support team that responds quickly to inquiries, resolving issues efficiently and showing a commitment to addressing customer needs promptly.

Assurance:

The competence, courtesy, credibility, and the ability to inspire confidence in customers. For example, a healthcare provider that not only offers medical services but also communicates effectively with patients, providing clear information about their health and treatment plans, instilling confidence in the care they receive.

Empathy:

The ability of service providers to understand and share the feelings of their customers. For example, a luxury hotel that goes beyond fulfilling basic needs and anticipates guest preferences, creating a personalized and empathetic experience that exceeds expectations.

Tangibles:

The physical appearance of facilities, equipment, personnel, and communication materials. For example, an airline that invests in modern and well-maintained aircraft, comfortable seating, and professional-looking staff to create a positive and tangible impression on passengers.

Courtesy:

Politeness, respect, consideration, and friendliness of contact personnel. For example, a retail store where employees greet customers warmly, provide assistance with a positive attitude, and create a friendly shopping environment.

Communication:

Keeping customers informed in a clear and understandable manner. For example: An internet service provider that communicates service outages in advance, providing regular updates to customers on the status of the issue and the expected resolution time.

Problem Resolution:

The ability of a service provider to address and resolve issues effectively. For example, an e-commerce platform that has a user-friendly return and refund process, efficiently handling customer complaints and ensuring a hassle-free resolution of problems.

By excelling in these dimensions, businesses can enhance service quality and, consequently, achieve higher levels of customer satisfaction. It's essential to continuously assess and improve these aspects to adapt to changing customer expectations and market dynamics.

SERVICE QUALITY GAP: (April, 2023; Nov. 2022)

The service gap model, also known as the SERVQUAL model, was developed by A. Parasuraman, Valarie Zeithaml, and Leonard Berry. It identifies the gaps that can occur during the service delivery process, leading to a difference between customer expectations and perceptions. The model outlines five key gaps that can impact service quality, explained as under:

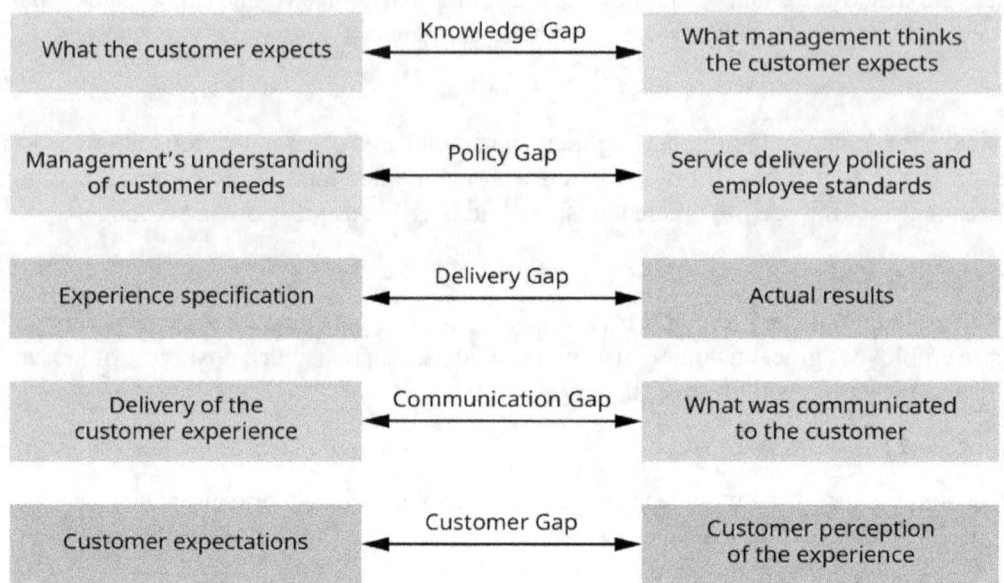

Gap 1: Knowledge Gap (Lack of Understanding Customer Expectations):

This gap exists when there is a difference between customer expectations and management perceptions of those expectations. For example, a restaurant manager believes customers primarily value the speed of service, while customers actually prioritize the quality of the food and atmosphere. This misalignment can lead to a gap between customer expectations and the management's understanding.

Gap 2: Policy Gap (Inadequate Service Quality Specifications):

This gap arises when management fails to translate accurate customer expectations into service quality specifications and standards. For example, a hotel promises luxurious rooms and amenities but fails to establish clear standards for housekeeping and maintenance. As a result, there may be inconsistencies in the quality of rooms, leading to a gap between service quality specifications and actual service delivery.

Gap 3: Delivery Gap (Failure to Meet Service Quality Specifications):

This gap occurs when there is a difference between service quality specifications and the service actually delivered. For example, a telecommunications company advertises 24/7 customer support, but in reality, customers often experience long wait times and inefficient problem resolution. The gap here is between what was promised and what was actually delivered.

Gap 4: Communication Gap (Ineffective Communication with Customers):

This gap arises when there is a difference between what is communicated to customers and what is actually delivered. For example, an airline advertises a commitment to on-time departures, but due to operational challenges, many flights are delayed. This creates a communication gap, as the service delivery does not align with the promises made in marketing communications.

Gap 5: Perception Gap (Difference Between Customer Expectations and Perceptions):

This gap represents the ultimate difference between customer expectations and perceptions of the service received. For example, a retail store promises a hassle-free return policy, but when a customer tries to return a product, they encounter difficulties and delays. The perception gap occurs when the customer's expectations of a smooth return process are not met.

To close these gaps and improve service quality, businesses need to focus on aligning management perceptions with customer expectations, establishing clear service quality specifications, ensuring consistent service delivery, improving communication with customers, and regularly assessing and addressing perception gaps. Continuous monitoring and adjustment in these areas can help businesses provide services that better meet customer expectations and enhance overall satisfaction.

IMPORTANCE OF RESEARCH FOR IMPROVING SERVICE QUALITY:

Research plays a crucial role in improving service quality by providing insights into customer needs, preferences, and expectations. It helps businesses identify areas where they can enhance their services, address gaps, and stay competitive in the market. The several ways in which research is important for improving service quality, are shown as under:

Understanding Customer Expectations:

Research allows businesses to gather information about what customers expect from their services. By understanding these expectations, companies can align their offerings with customer needs. For example, a hotel may conduct surveys and feedback sessions to learn that their guests prioritize cleanliness, efficient check-in processes, and friendly staff interactions. Armed with this knowledge, the hotel can focus on improving these specific aspects to meet and exceed guest expectations.

Identifying Service Gaps:

Research helps in identifying gaps between customer expectations and the actual service delivery. Recognizing these gaps is crucial for making targeted improvements and closing the divide between what customers want and what is being provided. For example, a restaurant might use mystery shoppers or customer feedback to identify gaps in service, such as slow response times from waitstaff. By addressing these issues, the restaurant can enhance the overall dining experience for its customers.

Benchmarking Against Competitors:

Research enables businesses to benchmark their service quality against industry standards and competitors. This comparison provides valuable insights into areas where a company may lag or excel, guiding improvement efforts. For example, an airline might conduct research to compare its on-time performance, in-flight services, and customer satisfaction ratings with those of its competitors. This information can guide the airline in making strategic improvements to stay competitive.

Innovating and Adapting to Changing Needs:

Research helps businesses stay informed about evolving customer preferences and industry trends. This information is crucial for adapting services to meet changing needs and for innovating to stay ahead of the competition. For example, a technology company researching customer preferences may discover a growing demand for mobile app features that streamline user experiences. By integrating these features, the company can enhance its service quality and better meet customer expectations.

Continuous Improvement:

Research provides a foundation for continuous improvement initiatives. By regularly collecting and analyzing data, businesses can identify trends, track performance over time, and make informed decisions to enhance service quality continually. For example, a retail chain may use customer feedback and sales data to identify areas for improvement in its online shopping experience. Regular research allows the company to make iterative changes to its website, checkout process, and customer service, leading to ongoing improvements.

WALKER CUSTOMER LOYALTY MATRIX

Walker's Loyalty Matrix is a framework for measuring loyalty and assessing the stability of an organization's customer base. Frameworks are useful as they provide a practical way to better understand business strategies. In the case of the Loyalty Matrix, it is a versatile approach, providing businesses with a practical means to leverage the voice of the customer for improved business performance.

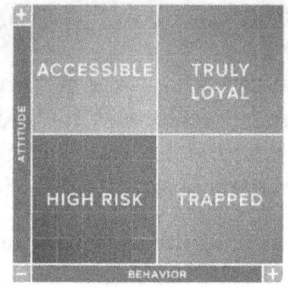

The Walker Loyalty Matrix is structured so the two axes represent the two aspects of loyalty – attitude and behavior. This forms four quadrants that can be defined as follows:

Truly Loyal:

These customers have every intention of continuing to do business with you and they have a positive attitude toward your company. They like working with you and are more likely to increase their spending and recommend your company to others.

Accessible:

These customers have a good attitude about working with you, but do not plan to continue their relationship. Since this is a rather odd combination, it's not surprising that it is often a very small percentage of customers. What it typically means is that something has changed in their business and they do not need your product or service any longer. However, they are often good advocates and will typically speak highly of your company.

Trapped:

These customers show every indication of continuing business with you, but they're not very happy about it. They feel trapped in the relationship. This is common among organizations locked into long-term contracts, lacking a suitable substitute, or finding that it is too hard to switch. Eventually, trapped customers will find a better option and are not likely to continue or increase business with you.

High Risk:

As the name implies, these customers do not intend to return and do not have a healthy attitude about their relationship with your company. Typically, they are halfway out the door and not only will they no longer be a customer, but will also talk poorly about you in the marketplace. This breakdown provides a very practical and flexible way of segmenting customers. For each of these quadrants specific action plans can be drawn to dramatically improve business performance.

3E's MEASURES OF CRM: (EFFICIENCY, EFFECTIVENESS AND EMPLOYEE CHANGE) (April, 2019)

Efficiency:

Efficiency in CRM refers to how well an organization utilizes its resources to manage and maintain customer relationships. It involves minimizing the time, effort, and cost required to deliver quality customer service and support. For example, a company implements a CRM system that streamlines data entry, automates routine tasks, and enables quick access to customer information. This enhances the efficiency of customer interactions, reducing the time it takes for employees to respond to customer inquiries.

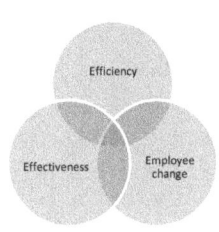

Effectiveness:

Effectiveness in CRM focuses on the ability of the organization to achieve its goals and objectives concerning customer relationships. It measures how well the CRM strategies and processes contribute to customer satisfaction, loyalty, and overall business success. For example, an e-commerce company introduces a personalized recommendation engine based on customer purchase history. This enhances the effectiveness of their CRM efforts by providing customers with relevant product suggestions, thereby increasing the likelihood of additional purchases.

Employee Change:

Employee change in the context of CRM refers to the extent to which the organization's employees embrace and adapt to new CRM strategies, technologies, or cultural shifts aimed at improving customer relationships. For example, a company undergoes a cultural transformation to become more customer-centric. Employees receive training on customer service best practices, and the company encourages a mindset shift towards prioritizing customer satisfaction. The degree to which employees embrace and embody this change is a measure of the effectiveness of CRM initiatives.

QUESTIONS:

Multiple-choice questions:

a) Long term CRM involves _____ operational cost. (Nov. 19)
   (i)High (ii) Low (iii) Medium (iv) None
b) _____ is the heart of selling process. (Nov. 19)
   (i)Customer delight (ii) Customer satisfaction (iii) Customer retention (iv) Customer loyalty
c) _____ is also known as opportunity management. (Nov. 19)
   (i)Customer relationship management (ii) Lead management (iii) Contact management (iv) Knowledge management
d) Privacy laws protect the interest of _____.(Nov. 19)
   (i)Customers (ii) Employees (iii) Organizations (iv) Business enterprises
e) _____ measure customer satisfaction, and therefore help to determine customer loyalty.

Customer Relationship Management

  (i) Customer representative (ii) Customer Service (iii) Customer Satisfaction Survey (iv) Customer EPOS

f) _____ indicates the difference between the service expected by customers and the service they receive.
   (i) Customer representative gap (ii) Customer Service (iii) Service quality gap (iv) Customer EPOS

g) _____ is an unpleasable fulfilment response.
   (i) Customer Service gap (ii) Service quality gap (iii) Customer EPOS (iv) Dissatisfaction

h) _____ model suggests that if customers perceive the expectations to be met, they are satisfied.
   (i) No expectations-confirmation (ii) Expectations-Disconfirmation (iii) Expectations-confirmation (iv) Expectations-satisfaction

i) Company 3E measure does not include _____. (Oct. 18)
   (i) effectiveness (ii) endurance (iii) employee change (iv) efficiency

Answers:- (a – i), (b - iii), (c - ii), (d – iv), (e - iii), (f - iii), (g - iv), (h - ii), (i - ii)

Fill in the blanks:

a) _____ helps the organization to increase the profitability at less operating cost.
b) _____ CRM helps a customer at many retail outlets loyalty programs through individual mobile phone.
c) _____ chain is designed in the 1990s to show the exact relationship and interconnectivity between Satisfaction – Loyalty – Retention and Profits, whereby it directly links to CRM.
d) CRM strategy cycle comprises of customer acquisition, retention and _____.
e) ERP stands for _____. (Oct., 2018)
f) _____ is a business statement that summarize why a customer should buy a particular product.
g) In CRM implementation Process, _____ is the last stage to check whether the goal has been achieved or not.
h) Quality = Customer's perception - _____.
i) The gap model is also known as the _____ of service quality.
j) _____ is the customer's fulfilment response to customer experience, or some part thereof.
k) _____ is all about attracting the right customer, getting them to buy, buy often, buy in higher quantities and bring more customers to the firm.

Answers:- CRM, (b) Mobile, (c) Company Profit chain, (d) Win-Back, (e) Entrepreneur resource planning, (f) Customer lifetime value, (g) CRM Evaluation, (h) Customer's expectations, (i) "5 gaps model", (j) Customer satisfaction, (k) Customer loyalty

True or False:

a) The cost of acquiring a customer is five times the cost of retaining an existing customer.
b) Customer lifetime value represents how much a customer is worth in terms of monetary value. (Oct. 18)
c) Customer win-back is a key element to CRM strategy.
d) Up-selling is a fairly established strategy for customer expansion, whereby one sells other products and services to existing customers.

e) Salesforce automation involves converting manual sales activities to electronic processes through the use of various combinations of hardware and software applications. (Oct. 18)
f) Customer retention is the first step in the CRM strategy cycle. (Oct. 18)
g) The service quality gap indicates the difference between the service expected by customers and the service they receive. (Oct. 18)
h) Satisfaction is an essential part of any business that wants to offer products or services that are focused and well-targeted.
i) Dissatisfaction is an unpleasant fulfilment response.
j) Expectations-Disconfirmation model suggests that if customers perceive their expectations to be met, they are satisfied.
k) Multimedia contact means well-organized contact data, viz. communication with clients, meetings, calls, email, as well as interactions through websites.
l) Once the survey design issues have been determined, the survey should not be pre-tested.

Answers:- (a) True, (b) True, (c) True, (d) False, (e) True, (f) False, (g) True, (h) False, (i) True, (j) True, (k) False, (l) False

Match the Following:

Group 'A'	Group 'B'
(a) Customer acquisition	(i) Saves new customer acquisition cost
(b) Customer expansion	(ii) Satisfaction-Loyalty-Profit chain
(c) Customer satisfaction	(iii) Lead management
(d) Customer loyalty	(iv) Cross-selling
(e) Gap 1	(v) The gap between management perception and the actual specification of the customer experience.
(f) Gap 2	(vi) The Gap between experience specification to the delivery of the experience.
(g) Gap 3	(vii) The gap between what customers expect and what service providers think they expect
(h) Gap 4	(viii) The gap between a customer's perception of the experience and the customer's expectation of the service.
(i) Gap 5	(ix) The gap between the delivery of the customer experience and what is communicated to customers.

Answers:- (a-iii), (b-iv), (c-i), (d-ii), (e-vii), (f-v), (g-vi), (h-ix), (i-viii)

Long answer type questions:

Q. what is customer value? Explain sales force automation with suitable examples. (April, 2023; April, 2019)

Q. Discuss planning and implementation of CRM. (April, 2023; Nov. 2019; April, 2019; Nov, 2018)

Q. Explain the company profit chain (April, 2023)

Q. Discuss the strategies to fill the service gaps. (April, 2023; Nov. 2022)

Customer Relationship Management

Q. What are the objectives of CRM strategy (Nov. 2022; Nov. 2018)

Q. Write a short note on contact management. (Nov. 2022)

Q. What are the complexities of CRM strategy. (Nov. 2019)

Q. Explain CRM strategy cycle (Nov. 2019; April, 2019)

Q. Explain the concept of knowledge management. (Nov. 2019; Nov. 2018)

Q. Bring out the relevance of 3E in CRM. (April, 2019)

Q. Explain B2B and sales in CRM.

UNIT 4: CRM NEW HORIZONS

- ✓ E-CRM
- ✓ Levels of E-CRM
- ✓ Six e's of E-CRM (process of E-CRM)
- ✓ Problems with E-CRM implementation
- ✓ E-CRM techniques used by banks in India
- ✓ Privacy issues in E-CRM
- ✓ Solutions for privacy issues
- ✓ Service automation in CRM
- ✓ Service automation software applications for customer service
    1. Activity management
    2. Agent management
    3. Case assignment
    4. Case management
    5. Contract management
    6. Customer self-service
    7. Email response management
    8. Escalation
    9. Inbound communication management
    10. Invoicing
    11. Outbound communication management
    12. Queuing and routing
    13. Scheduling
- ✓ Social networking and CRM
- ✓ Mobile CRM

Customer Relationship Management

> - ✓ Global CRM
> - ✓ Recent trends in CRM
> - ✓ Challenges faced by CRM
> - ✓ Opportunities for CRM
> - ✓ Ethical issues in CRM
> - ✓ Questions

E-CRM (April, 2023; Nov., 2022; Nov., 2019; April, 2019; Nov., 2018)

Electronic Customer Relationship Management (e-CRM) refers to the integration of customer relationship management processes with electronic technologies. It involves using digital tools and platforms to manage, analyze, and improve interactions between a company and its customers. The few examples of E-CRM are shown as under:

Salesforce is a widely used e-CRM platform that offers a range of tools for managing customer relationships, sales, and marketing. It allows businesses to track leads, analyze customer data, and automate various processes.

HubSpot provides an integrated platform for inbound marketing, sales, and customer service. It includes features for email marketing, lead nurturing, and customer analytics.

Zendesk is known for its customer service solutions. It helps businesses manage customer support inquiries, automate responses, and gather insights to improve overall customer satisfaction.

Benefits of E-CRM:

Improved Customer Understanding:

E-CRM systems allow businesses to gather and analyze customer data effectively. This data can include purchase history, preferences, and behavior, providing a deeper understanding of customer needs.

Personalization:

With the insights gained from E-CRM, businesses can tailor their marketing and communication strategies. Personalized offers, recommendations, and targeted messages enhance the customer experience and increase engagement.

Efficient Communication:

E-CRM facilitates seamless communication with customers through various digital channels, such as email, social media, and chat. This helps in responding to customer queries promptly and building a stronger relationship.

Streamlined Sales Processes:

Automation features in e-CRM systems streamline sales processes, from lead generation to closing deals. This efficiency allows sales teams to focus on building relationships rather than administrative tasks.

Customer Retention and Loyalty:

By understanding customer preferences and addressing their needs, businesses can foster loyalty. E-CRM helps in creating loyalty programs, targeted promotions, and follow-up strategies to retain customers over the long term.

Disadvantages of E-CRM:

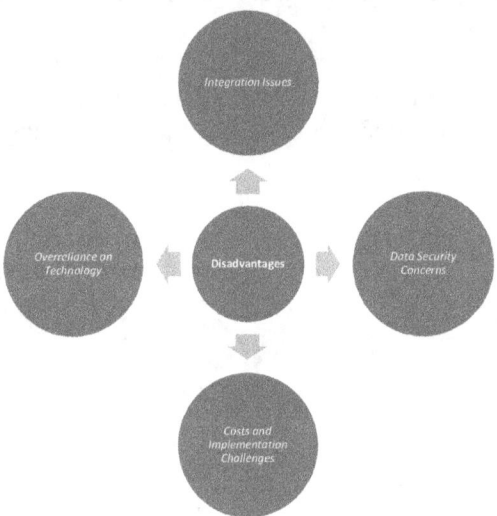

Costs and Implementation Challenges:

Implementing e-CRM systems can be expensive, requiring initial investments in software, hardware, and training. Small businesses may find it challenging to allocate resources for this purpose.

Data Security Concerns:

With the collection and storage of vast amounts of customer data, there are concerns about data security. Businesses need to invest in robust security measures to protect customer information from unauthorized access and breaches.

Integration Issues:

Integration with existing systems and databases can be complex. Incompatibility issues may arise, leading to disruptions in business operations during the implementation phase.

Overreliance on Technology:

While e-CRM enhances efficiency, an overreliance on technology might lead to a loss of personal touch in customer interactions. Balancing automation with personalized communication is crucial.

LEVELS OF E-CRM

Electronic Customer Relationship Management (e-CRM) can be understood in different levels, each representing a stage of interaction and relationship-building with customers.

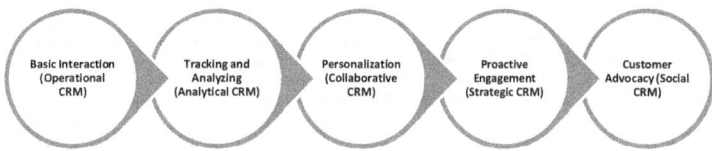

Level 1: Basic Interaction (Operational CRM):

This level involves basic customer interactions and focuses on streamlining day-to-day operations. For example, using a system to manage customer contacts, track sales leads, and automate routine tasks. It ensures smooth operational processes.

Level 2: Tracking and Analyzing (Analytical CRM):

Here, businesses start analyzing customer data to gain insights and make informed decisions. For example, analyzing customer buying patterns to identify trends, preferences, and areas for improvement in products or services.

Level 3: Personalization (Collaborative CRM):

This level emphasizes collaboration and personalized interactions with customers. For example, implementing systems for customer feedback, reviews, and social media engagement to understand individual preferences and tailor services accordingly.

Level 4: Proactive Engagement (Strategic CRM):

Businesses take a proactive approach, anticipating customer needs and providing personalized solutions. For example, using predictive analytics to forecast customer behavior, enabling businesses to offer targeted promotions or recommendations in advance.

Level 5: Customer Advocacy (Social CRM):

The highest level involves building strong relationships, encouraging customer loyalty, and turning customers into advocates. For example, leveraging social media to create communities, where satisfied customers become brand advocates, sharing positive experiences and recommendations.

SIX E's OF E-CRM (PROCESS OF E-CRM)

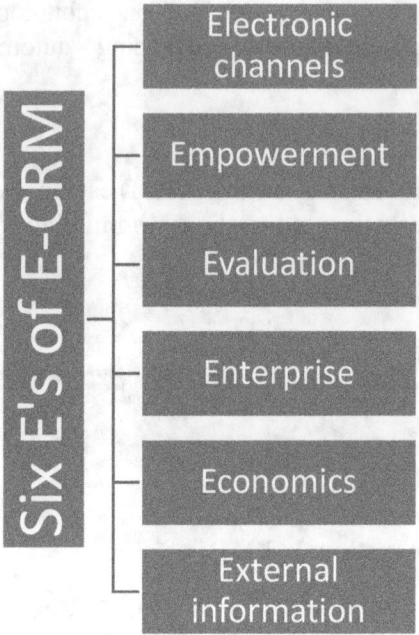

1. Electronic Channels:

Understand and explore customer needs and preferences through various electronic channels. For example, utilizing online platforms like social media, email, and website analytics to gather insights. For instance, a retail business might explore customer behavior on their website to identify popular products or improve the user experience.

2. Empowerment:

Engage and excite customers by empowering them with the tools and resources to take control of their interactions. For example, providing self-service options, FAQs, or online support portals. An empowered customer can, for example, customize their preferences in an online account or troubleshoot issues without direct assistance.

3. Evaluation:

Provide customers with information and education about products or services, and evaluate the effectiveness of these efforts. For example, implementing customer feedback mechanisms, surveys, and analyzing the success of educational content. For instance, a software company might evaluate the impact of tutorial videos on customer satisfaction and product usage.

4. Enterprise:

Focus on creating positive and memorable customer experiences by aligning e-CRM efforts with the broader enterprise goals. For example, integrating e-CRM systems with other enterprise systems such as ERP (Enterprise Resource Planning) to ensure a seamless flow of information. For example, a retail enterprise might integrate e-CRM with inventory management to optimize stock levels based on customer demand.

5. Economics:

Actively involve customers in the brand or product through two-way communication and consider the economic implications of these engagements. For example, analyzing the return on investment (ROI) of e-CRM initiatives, considering factors like customer acquisition costs

Customer Relationship Management

and lifetime value. A subscription-based service, for instance, might engage customers by offering exclusive content, and the economic analysis would assess the impact on customer retention and revenue.

6. **External Information**:

Empower customers by giving them the tools, resources, or support they need, and leverage external information to enhance customer interactions. For example, utilizing external data sources, such as market trends and competitor analysis, to inform e-CRM strategies. For instance, a fashion retailer might empower customers with personalized style recommendations based on external fashion trends and preferences.

PROBLEMS WITH E-CRM IMPLEMENTATION

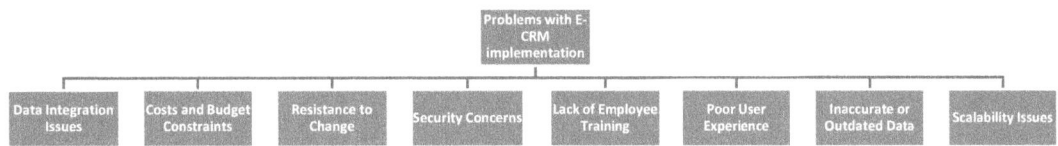

Implementing e-CRM (Electronic Customer Relationship Management) can face various challenges which are discussed as under:

Data Integration Issues:

Difficulty in integrating e-CRM systems with existing databases and software. For example, a company may face challenges when trying to connect its customer database with a new e-CRM platform, leading to data inconsistencies and errors.

Costs and Budget Constraints:

High implementation costs and budget limitations can hinder the adoption of e-CRM. For example, small businesses might find it challenging to allocate sufficient funds for the purchase of e-CRM software licenses and the necessary infrastructure.

Resistance to Change:

Employees may resist adapting to new e-CRM processes, leading to slow adoption. For example, staff members may prefer traditional methods of customer interaction and be resistant to using new digital tools, impacting the effectiveness of the e-CRM implementation.

Security Concerns:

Concerns about data security and privacy may arise, particularly when dealing with sensitive customer information. For example, a healthcare organization implementing e-CRM needs to ensure strict security measures to protect patient data, preventing unauthorized access.

Lack of Employee Training:

Inadequate training for employees on how to use the new e-CRM tools can hinder effective implementation. For example, without proper training, customer service representatives may struggle to navigate the e-CRM system, leading to delays and frustration in customer interactions.

Poor User Experience:

If the e-CRM system is not user-friendly, it can result in low adoption rates and dissatisfaction among users. For example, a company implements a complex e-CRM interface without considering user experience, leading to employees struggling to find necessary information and perform tasks efficiently.

Inaccurate or Outdated Data:

Inaccuracies in customer data or reliance on outdated information can impact decision-making. For example, if the e-CRM system doesn't regularly update customer profiles, marketing efforts may be based on outdated preferences, leading to less effective targeting.

Scalability Issues:

E-CRM systems may face challenges in scaling up to handle increased data volumes as a business grows. For example, a successful marketing campaign generates a surge in customer interactions, and the e-CRM system struggles to handle the increased load, resulting in delays and potential data loss.

E-CRM TECHNIQUES USED BY BANKS IN INDIA

Electronic Customer Relationship Management (e-CRM) techniques used by banks in India involve the use of digital tools and technologies to enhance customer interactions, improve services, and build stronger relationships. Some common techniques used by banks are explained as under:

Online Banking Portals:

Banks provide secure online portals that enable customers to perform various banking activities such as checking account balances, transferring funds, paying bills, and managing investments. For example, State Bank of India (SBI) offers an extensive online banking platform, allowing customers to access a wide range of banking services through their website and mobile app.

Mobile Banking Apps:

Banks develop user-friendly mobile applications that allow customers to perform banking transactions on their smartphones or tablets. For example, ICICI Bank's Mobile app provides features like fund transfers, bill payments, and account management, enhancing convenience for customers on the go.

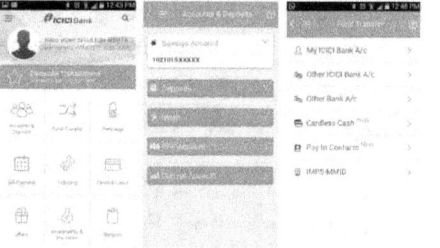

SMS and Email Alerts:

Customer Relationship Management

Banks use SMS and email notifications to keep customers informed about their account activities, transactions, and important updates. For example, HDFC Bank sends SMS alerts for every transaction made with the account, providing real-time updates to customers about their financial activities.

Chatbots for Customer Support:

Many banks deploy AI-driven chatbots on their websites and mobile apps to provide instant customer support and answer queries. For example, Axis Bank's chatbot, Axis Aha!, assists customers with account-related inquiries, product information, and general banking queries.

Personalized Marketing Campaigns:

Banks use customer data to create targeted marketing campaigns, offering personalized product recommendations, promotions, and special offers. For example, Kotak Mahindra Bank may send personalized loan offers to customers based on their transaction history and financial behavior.

Social Media Engagement:

Banks leverage social media platforms to engage with customers, address concerns, and share information about new services or promotions. For example, Yes Bank uses platforms like Twitter and Facebook to interact with customers, provide updates, and gather feedback.

Customer Feedback Surveys:

Banks conduct online surveys to gather feedback from customers, allowing them to understand satisfaction levels and identify areas for improvement. For example, Punjab National Bank (PNB) may send out surveys to customers via email to gather insights on their experiences with the bank's services.

Customer Relationship Analytics:

Banks use analytics tools to analyze customer behavior, preferences, and transaction patterns, helping in making data-driven decisions. For example, Canara Bank might use analytics to identify trends in customer spending and offer targeted financial advice or product suggestions.

PRIVACY ISSUES IN E-CRM: (Nov., 2022; Nov., 2018)

Privacy is a significant concern in Electronic Customer Relationship Management (e-CRM) as it involves the collection, storage, and analysis of customer data. Following are few issues in E-CRM.

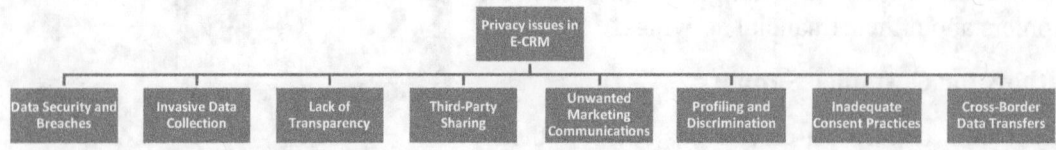

Data Security and Breaches:

Inadequate security measures can lead to unauthorized access and data breaches, compromising customer privacy. For example, a cyberattack on a bank's e-CRM system may result in the exposure of customer information, including personal details and financial transactions.

Invasive Data Collection:

Excessive and intrusive data collection practices may infringe on customer privacy. For example, a retail e-commerce site collecting more information than necessary, such as tracking users' browsing history across unrelated websites, without clear consent.

Lack of Transparency:

Customers may be unaware of how their data is being used or may lack transparency about the purposes of data collection. For example, a social media platform using algorithms to analyze user behavior for targeted advertising without clearly informing users about the extent of data utilization.

Third-Party Sharing:

Sharing customer data with third parties without explicit consent can lead to privacy concerns. For example, a telecommunications company selling customer call records to advertisers without the knowledge or consent of the customers.

Unwanted Marketing Communications:

Unsolicited and intrusive marketing messages may result from the misuse of customer contact information. For example, sending excessive promotional emails to customers based on their purchase history without providing an option to opt out.

Profiling and Discrimination:

The use of customer data for profiling may lead to unfair discrimination or exclusion of certain groups. For example, a financial institution using demographic data to determine creditworthiness may inadvertently discriminate against individuals from specific ethnic or socioeconomic backgrounds.

Inadequate Consent Practices:

Obtaining consent from customers may not always be clear, informed, or specific, leading to privacy concerns. For example, a mobile app requesting broad permissions during installation without explaining why each permission is needed, leaving users unsure about the extent of data access.

Customer Relationship Management

Cross-Border Data Transfers:

When customer data is transferred across borders, it may be subject to different privacy laws, potentially compromising the protection of customer information. For example, an e-commerce company storing customer data on servers located in a country with less stringent privacy regulations than the customer's home country.

SOLUTIONS FOR PRIVACY ISSUES: (Nov., 2022; Nov., 2018)

Addressing privacy issues in Electronic Customer Relationship Management (e-CRM) involves implementing robust solutions to protect customer data and ensure compliance with privacy regulations. Following are some solution to deal with privacy issues:

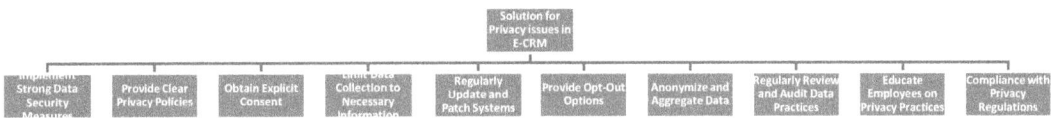

Implement Strong Data Security Measures:

Employ encryption, access controls, and secure authentication methods to safeguard customer data. For example, a bank using end-to-end encryption for online transactions, ensuring that sensitive financial information is securely transmitted and stored.

Provide Clear Privacy Policies:

Clearly communicate how customer data is collected, used, and shared through easily accessible and transparent privacy policies. For example, an e-commerce website displaying a concise and easily understandable privacy policy on its homepage, detailing data collection practices and purposes.

Obtain Explicit Consent:

Ensure that customers provide explicit and informed consent before collecting and processing their data. For example, an email marketing platform requiring users to opt-in and confirm their subscription before receiving promotional emails, ensuring explicit consent.

Limit Data Collection to Necessary Information:

Collect only the data necessary for the intended purpose and avoid unnecessary or invasive data collection. For example, an online survey platform requesting only essential demographic information needed for the survey, without asking for irrelevant details.

Regularly Update and Patch Systems:

Keep e-CRM systems up to date with the latest security patches to prevent vulnerabilities that could be exploited. For example, a software company regularly releasing updates for its CRM platform, including security patches to address potential vulnerabilities.

Provide Opt-Out Options:

Allow customers to opt out of certain data collection or marketing communications. For example, a newsletter subscription service including an easy-to-find "unsubscribe" link in every email, allowing users to opt out of receiving further communications.

Anonymize and Aggregate Data:

Aggregate and anonymize customer data whenever possible to protect individual identities. For example, a market research company combining survey responses in a way that removes personally identifiable information, ensuring the privacy of respondents.

Regularly Review and Audit Data Practices:

Conduct regular reviews and audits of data practices to identify and rectify potential privacy risks. For example, an online platform for financial transactions conducting periodic internal audits to ensure compliance with data protection regulations.

Educate Employees on Privacy Practices:

Train employees on the importance of privacy, data protection policies, and the secure handling of customer information. For example, a telecommunications company conducting regular employee training sessions on data privacy and security protocols.

Compliance with Privacy Regulations:

Stay informed about and comply with relevant privacy regulations, such as GDPR or local data protection laws. For example, a multinational e-commerce platform adapting its data practices to comply with different privacy regulations in various countries where it operates.

SERVICE AUTOMATION IN CRM

Service automation in CRM (Customer Relationship Management) refers to the use of technology and software tools to automate various processes related to customer service and support. This includes streamlining tasks, improving efficiency, and enhancing the overall customer experience. Service automation in CRM typically involves automating activities such as issue resolution, ticket management, and communication with customers. The features of service automation in CRM are as under:

Customer Relationship Management

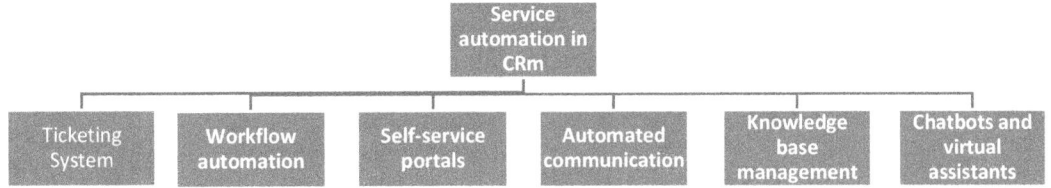

Ticketing System:

Automated systems for logging, tracking, and managing customer issues or service requests. For example, a helpdesk system that automatically assigns tickets to relevant support agents based on predefined rules and priorities.

Workflow Automation:

Automated workflows that guide and streamline the resolution process for common service tasks. For example, an automated workflow that triggers a series of predefined actions when a customer submits a service request, such as assigning tasks, sending notifications, and updating records.

Self-Service Portals:

Online platforms or portals that allow customers to find answers to common queries or resolve issues independently. For example, a customer portal where users can access FAQs, knowledge base articles, and troubleshooting guides to address common issues without the need for direct support.

Automated Communication:

Automated communication tools for sending updates, notifications, and responses to customers. For example, automated email notifications to customers informing them about the status of their service request or providing follow-up information after a support interaction.

Knowledge Base Management:

Centralized repositories of information that agents can use to access and share knowledge for issue resolution. For example, a knowledge base system that automatically suggests relevant articles or solutions to support agents based on the details of a customer inquiry.

Chatbots and Virtual Assistants:

AI-powered tools that can engage with customers in real-time, answer questions, and assist with common service tasks. For example, a chatbot integrated into a CRM system that handles routine customer inquiries, gathers information, and provides initial assistance before routing complex issues to human agents.

Benefits of Service Automation in CRM:

1. Automation reduces manual effort, allowing service teams to handle a higher volume of requests with greater efficiency.
2. Automation ensures quicker response times to customer inquiries and issues, contributing to improved customer satisfaction.
3. Automated processes ensure that service tasks are executed consistently, reducing the likelihood of errors or oversights.
4. Quick issue resolution, self-service options, and proactive communication contribute to an overall positive customer experience.
5. Service automation allows businesses to optimize resource allocation, ensuring that human agents focus on complex tasks while routine activities are handled by automated systems.

SERVICE AUTOMATION SOFTWARE APPLICATIONS FOR CUSTOMER SERVICE: (Nov., 2019)

There is a large number of service automation software applications available in the market. The applications which are discussed here are as under:

Activity Management:

Activity management tools help in organizing and tracking various tasks and activities related to customer service. For example, Trello is a popular activity management tool that allows customer service teams to create boards, lists, and cards to manage and track different tasks and activities.

Agent Management:

Customer Relationship Management

Agent management tools assist in managing and optimizing the performance of customer service agents. For example: Zendesk Support provides agent management features, allowing administrators to monitor agent activities, track performance metrics, and manage workloads effectively.

Case Assignment:

Case assignment tools automate the process of assigning customer cases or service requests to appropriate agents or teams. For example, Salesforce Service Cloud includes automated case assignment features based on predefined rules, ensuring that cases are routed to the right agents.

Case Management:

Case management software helps in tracking, resolving, and documenting customer issues or cases throughout their lifecycle. For example, Freshdesk offers a comprehensive case management system, allowing agents to log, track, and resolve customer issues efficiently.

Contract Management:

Contract management tools automate the creation, tracking, and management of service contracts with customers. For example, ContractSafe is a contract management platform that automates the storage, tracking, and renewal of service contracts.

Customer Self-Service:

Customer self-service tools enable customers to find solutions to their problems independently using knowledge bases, FAQs, and other resources. For example, HubSpot Service Hub provides a customer self-service portal where users can access articles, FAQs, and community forums for problem-solving.

Email Response Management: (April, 2023; Nov., 2022; Nov., 2019; Nov., 2018)

Email response management tools automate the handling and organization of incoming customer emails. For example, Front is an email collaboration platform that streamlines email responses by centralizing communication, assigning emails to agents, and providing collaboration features.

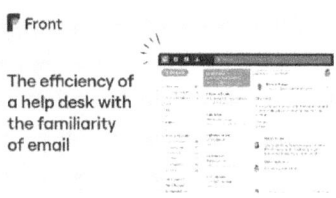

Escalation:

Description: Escalation tools automate the process of escalating customer issues to higher levels of support or management when needed. For example, Jira Service Management includes automated escalation workflows, ensuring that critical issues are escalated promptly to the appropriate level.

Inbound Communication Management: (April, 2023; April, 2019)

Inbound communication management tools organize and manage various forms of customer communication, such as messages, chats, and inquiries. For example, Intercom is a customer communication platform that helps businesses manage inbound communication through a unified inbox and automated routing.

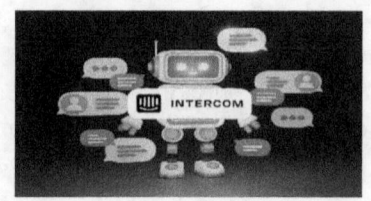

Invoicing:

Invoicing tools automate the generation and processing of invoices for services provided. For example, QuickBooks is an invoicing software that automates the creation, tracking, and management of invoices for services rendered to customers.

Outbound Communication Management:

Outbound communication management tools automate the scheduling and delivery of proactive communications to customers. For example, SendGrid is an email marketing platform that enables businesses to automate outbound communications such as newsletters, updates, and promotional emails.

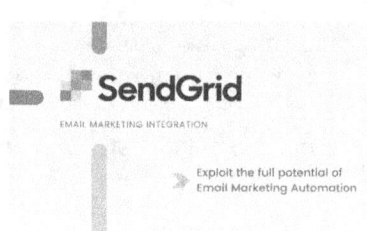

Queuing and Routing: (April, 2023)

Queuing and routing tools manage the distribution and routing of customer service requests to the appropriate agents or teams. For example, Genesys Cloud offers queuing and routing features that intelligently route customer inquiries to the most suitable available agents based on various criteria.

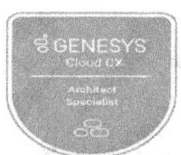

Scheduling:

Scheduling tools automate the process of setting appointments, meetings, or service interactions with customers. For example, Calendly is a scheduling tool that allows customers to book appointments with customer service representatives based on their availability.

SOCIAL NETWORKING AND CRM: (April, 2023; Nov., 2019; April, 2019; Nov., 2018)

Social networking and Customer Relationship Management (CRM) are two distinct concepts, but they can be interconnected to enhance customer engagement and relationships. Social networking involves the use of online platforms, such as Facebook, Twitter, LinkedIn, and Instagram, to connect and interact with individuals or groups. Users share information, engage in conversations, and build networks within these platforms.

On the other side, CRM is a business strategy and set of practices aimed at managing and improving relationships with customers. It involves collecting, analyzing, and leveraging customer data to enhance customer satisfaction, loyalty, and overall business performance.

Social CRM combines traditional CRM practices with social media to leverage social networking platforms for customer interaction and relationship-building. Social CRM involves monitoring and engaging with customers on social media channels, gathering insights from social interactions, and integrating this information into the CRM system to enhance the overall understanding of the customer.

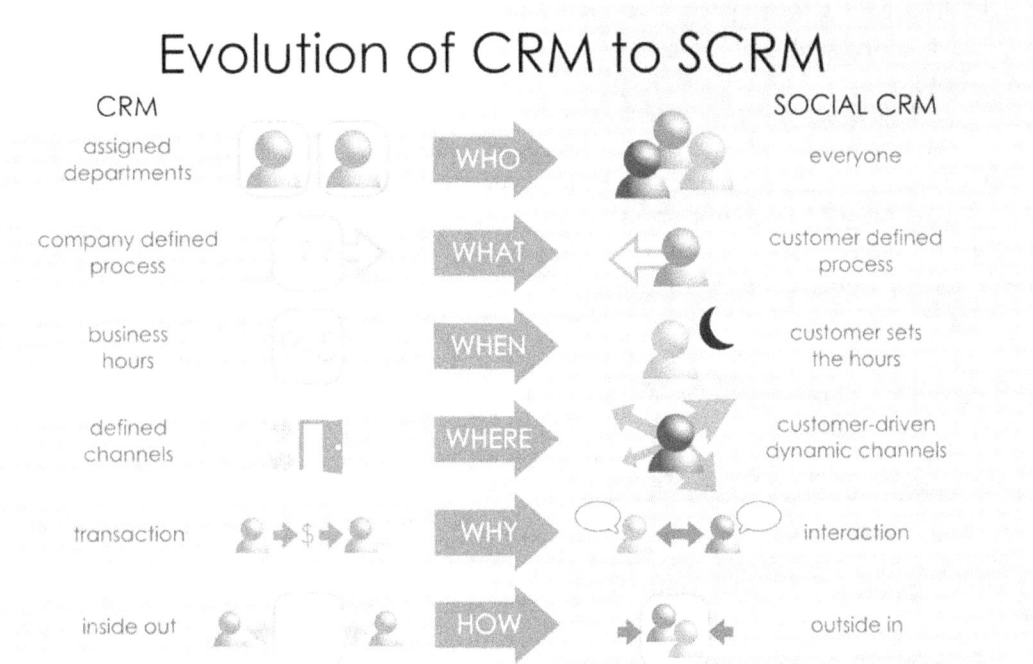

Benefits of Social CRM:

1. Social CRM allows businesses to actively engage with customers on social media platforms, responding to queries, addressing concerns, and participating in discussions.
2. By monitoring social media conversations, businesses can gain real-time insights into customer opinions, preferences, and trends, which can be valuable for refining products or services.
3. Social CRM enables businesses to create targeted marketing campaigns based on the information gathered from social media interactions, leading to more personalized and effective marketing strategies.
4. Engaging with customers on social media can turn satisfied customers into brand advocates, as positive interactions are often shared with a broader audience.

Challenges and Considerations:

1. Handling customer data on social media requires careful consideration of privacy regulations and ensuring that customer data is used ethically and securely.
2. Integrating social CRM with existing CRM systems can be complex, and businesses need to ensure a seamless flow of information between these platforms.
3. Maintaining a consistent brand voice and messaging across social media interactions and other customer touchpoints is crucial for a positive customer experience.

MOBILE CRM: (Nov., 2022; Nov., 2018)

Mobile Customer Relationship Management (CRM) refers to the use of mobile devices, such as smartphones and tablets, to manage and enhance customer relationships. Mobile CRM allows businesses to interact with customers, access important customer data, and perform CRM activities on the go. The important features of mobile CRM are as under:

1. Mobile CRM enables sales representatives, customer support agents, and other personnel to access crucial customer information anytime, anywhere. For example, a salesperson using a mobile CRM app to view a customer's purchase history, preferences, and recent interactions before a sales meeting.
2. Mobile CRM facilitates real-time communication and interaction with customers through various channels like calls, messages, and emails. For example, a customer support agent using a mobile CRM app to respond promptly to customer inquiries received via social media or email while on the move.
3. Sales representatives can use mobile CRM tools to manage leads, update deal statuses, and access product information while in the field. For example, a field salesperson using a mobile CRM app to update the status of a sales opportunity, add notes, and schedule follow-up tasks after a client meeting.
4. Mobile CRM can leverage GPS and location data to provide context-aware information and services based on the user's location. For example, a salesperson using location-based services in a mobile CRM app to identify nearby prospects and access relevant information for spontaneous client visits.
5. Mobile CRM apps often include features for scheduling and managing tasks, appointments, and events, helping users stay organized. For example, a customer service representative using a mobile CRM app to set reminders for follow-up calls, manage appointments, and prioritize tasks.
6. Some mobile CRM applications offer offline functionality, allowing users to access and update customer data even without an internet connection. For example, a salesperson using a mobile CRM app in an area with poor network coverage to review and update customer information, which will sync once a connection is restored.
7. Mobile CRM tools may integrate with communication apps, enabling seamless communication with customers through messaging and calling features. For example, an account manager using a mobile CRM app integrated with messaging apps to quickly communicate with clients and respond to urgent queries.
8. Mobile CRM platforms often include analytics and reporting features, allowing users to track key performance indicators and generate reports on the go. For example, a sales manager using a mobile CRM app to check real-time sales performance metrics and generate a sales report during a business trip.
9. Mobile CRM platforms prioritize security by implementing features like device authentication and encryption to protect sensitive customer data. For example, a financial advisor using a mobile CRM app that requires biometric authentication to access confidential client financial information.

GLOBAL CRM (April, 2019)

Global CRM, or Global Customer Relationship Management, refers to the strategies, processes, and technologies that companies use to manage and analyze their interactions with

Customer Relationship Management

customers across different regions and countries. CRM systems are designed to streamline and enhance customer relationships by providing a centralized database of customer information and interactions.

In a global context, businesses often operate in diverse markets with varying cultural, regulatory, and economic conditions. Global CRM aims to address these complexities and create a unified approach to managing customer relationships on a worldwide scale. This involves adapting CRM strategies to accommodate diverse customer preferences, languages, and business practices. Key features of global CRM may include:

1. The ability to interact with customers in their preferred languages is crucial for effective global CRM.
2. Integration of customer data from various sources and regions to create a comprehensive view of the customer across the organization.
3. Adherence to different data protection and privacy regulations in various countries to ensure legal and ethical handling of customer information.
4. Tailoring marketing strategies and campaigns to suit the cultural nuances and preferences of different regions.
5. While adapting to local needs, there is often a need for centralized control and management to ensure consistency and efficiency.
6. Coordinating communication across different channels and touchpoints to provide a seamless customer experience.

RECENT TRENDS IN CRM:

AI and Machine Learning Integration:

The integration of Artificial Intelligence (AI) and Machine Learning (ML) in CRM systems to automate tasks, analyze customer data for insights, and enhance predictive analytics. For example, Salesforce Einstein uses AI to provide personalized customer experiences, automate repetitive tasks, and offer predictive analytics for sales and marketing.

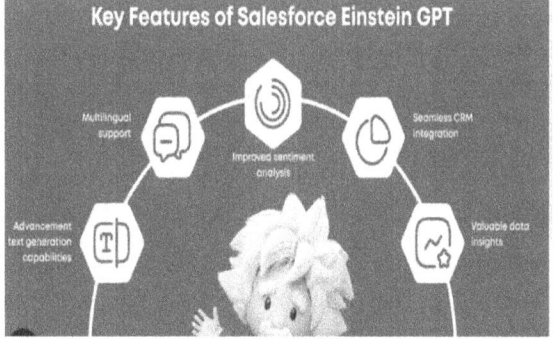

Customer Data Platform (CDP):

The adoption of Customer Data Platforms for unified, comprehensive customer data management across various touchpoints and channels. For example, Segment is a CDP that helps businesses collect, unify, and analyze customer data from various sources to create a unified customer profile.

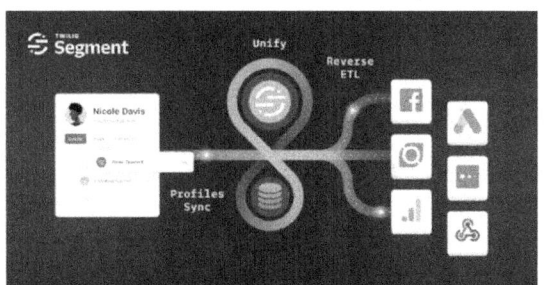

Voice Technology in CRM:

The use of voice-activated technologies and virtual assistants to facilitate hands-free interaction with CRM systems. For example, Zoho CRM Voice enables users to update records, make calls, and perform other CRM tasks using voice commands.

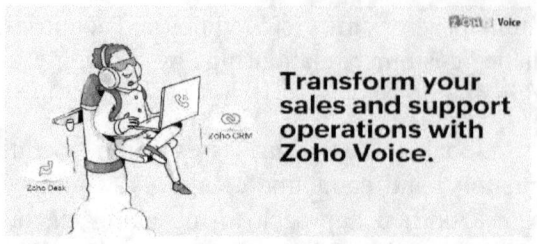

Conversational CRM:

The emphasis on conversational interfaces and messaging platforms for customer interactions, leveraging chatbots and live chat for real-time communication. For example, HubSpot's Conversations tool allows businesses to engage with customers through live chat, chatbots, and team email, all within a unified platform.

Personalization and Hyper-Personalization:

Increasing focus on delivering personalized experiences by tailoring marketing messages, product recommendations, and customer interactions based on individual preferences. For example, Amazon's personalized product recommendations and content recommendations based on user behavior and preferences.

Mobile CRM and Remote Accessibility:

The importance of mobile CRM applications for remote work and the need for CRM platforms to provide seamless access from various devices. For example, Microsoft Dynamics 365 offer mobile apps that allow users to access CRM functionalities on smartphones and tablets.

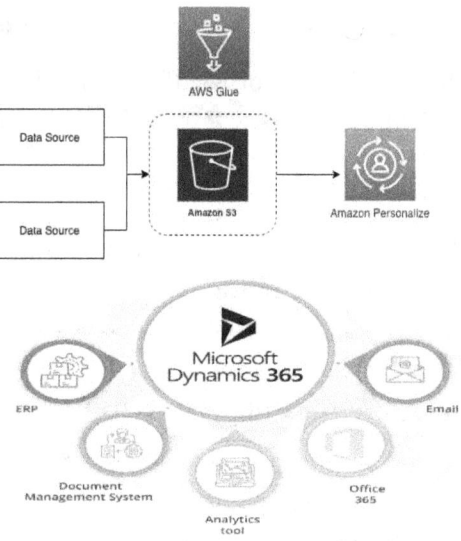

Integration with Collaboration Tools:

Integration of CRM systems with collaboration tools to streamline communication and facilitate collaboration among team members. For example, Slack integration with CRM platforms like Salesforce, enabling teams to receive CRM updates and collaborate within the messaging platform.

Social CRM and Social Listening:

Continued emphasis on Social CRM, leveraging social media data for customer insights and integrating social listening tools to monitor brand mentions. For example, Hootsuite integrates with CRM systems to help businesses monitor social media conversations, engage with customers, and gather insights.

CHALLENGES FACED BY CRM: (Nov. 2018)

Implementing Customer Relationship Management (CRM) systems can bring numerous benefits, but it also comes with its own set of challenges. Here are various challenges faced by CRM:

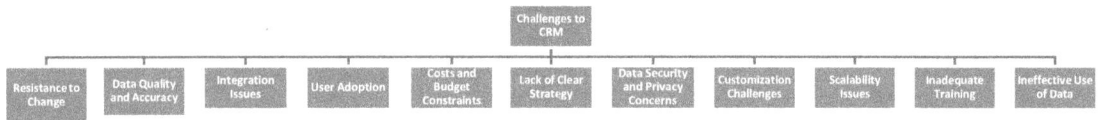

Resistance to Change:

Employees might resist adopting new CRM processes and technologies, particularly if they are accustomed to existing workflows. For example, sales representatives may be hesitant to shift from manual record-keeping to using a CRM system for tracking customer interactions.

Data Quality and Accuracy:

Maintaining clean, accurate, and up-to-date data can be challenging, especially when dealing with large volumes of customer information. For example, duplicate records, incomplete data, and outdated information can lead to inaccurate insights and hinder effective decision-making.

Integration Issues:

Integrating CRM systems with existing business applications and databases can be complex, leading to data silos and inconsistencies. For example, an organization may face challenges connecting its CRM system with the company's accounting or inventory management software.

User Adoption:

Encouraging users to fully embrace and utilize the CRM system can be difficult, impacting the system's effectiveness. For example, if employees find the CRM interface complex or time-consuming, they may revert to using their previous methods, reducing the system's adoption rate.

Costs and Budget Constraints:

Implementing and maintaining a CRM system can incur significant costs, and budget constraints may limit the choice of a robust solution. For example, small businesses may find it challenging to allocate sufficient funds for CRM software licenses, training, and ongoing support.

Lack of Clear Strategy:

Without a well-defined CRM strategy, organizations may struggle to align CRM efforts with business objectives. For example, a company might invest in a CRM system without a clear plan for how it will be used to improve customer relationships and drive business outcomes.

Data Security and Privacy Concerns:

Storing and managing sensitive customer data requires robust security measures to prevent unauthorized access and protect privacy. For example, a data breach in a CRM system could lead to the exposure of customer information, damaging trust and reputation.

Customization Challenges:

Customizing CRM systems to meet specific business needs may be complex and may require technical expertise. For example, a company may struggle to configure the CRM platform to match its unique sales processes and workflows.

Scalability Issues:

As a business grows, the CRM system must scale to accommodate increased data volumes and user demands. For example, a successful marketing campaign may generate a surge in customer interactions, and the CRM system must be able to handle the increased workload.

Inadequate Training:

Without proper training, employees may not fully understand the features and capabilities of the CRM system. For example, customer service representatives may not effectively use the CRM's ticketing system if they haven't received sufficient training on how to navigate and utilize it.

Ineffective Use of Data:

Even with a wealth of data, organizations may struggle to extract meaningful insights and utilize the information for strategic decision-making. For example, a company may collect customer data but fail to analyze it effectively to identify trends or personalize marketing campaigns.

OPPORTUNITIES FOR CRM (Nov., 2022; Nov., 2019)

Customer Relationship Management (CRM) presents numerous opportunities for businesses to improve customer interactions, enhance customer satisfaction, and drive overall business success. Few of these opportunities are discussed as under:

Customer Relationship Management

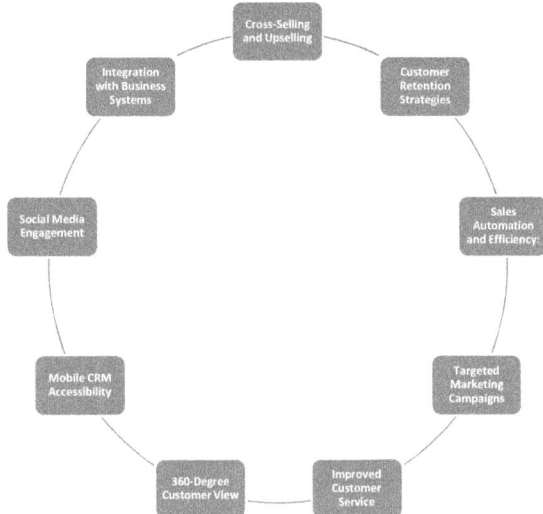

360-Degree Customer View:

A comprehensive understanding of customer behavior, preferences, and interactions allows businesses to provide personalized experiences. For example, Salesforce provides a 360-degree view of customers by consolidating data from various touchpoints, enabling businesses to tailor their interactions based on individual preferences.

Improved Customer Service:

CRM systems enable businesses to streamline customer service processes, respond to queries promptly, and enhance overall customer satisfaction. For example, Zendesk's CRM platform helps businesses provide efficient customer support by consolidating customer interactions, automating ticketing, and facilitating seamless communication.

Targeted Marketing Campaigns:

CRM data enables businesses to create targeted and personalized marketing campaigns, improving the relevance of communications. For example, HubSpot CRM allows businesses to segment their customer base and execute targeted email campaigns, ensuring that marketing messages are tailored to specific audience segments.

Sales Automation and Efficiency:

CRM systems automate sales processes, reducing manual tasks and improving the efficiency of sales teams. For example, Pipedrive is a CRM platform that automates sales workflows, helping sales teams manage leads, track deals, and streamline the sales pipeline.

Customer Retention Strategies:

CRM facilitates the implementation of customer retention strategies by identifying at-risk customers and tailoring retention efforts. For example, Retently is a customer feedback and retention platform that integrates with CRM systems, allowing businesses to measure customer satisfaction and implement retention strategies based on feedback.

Cross-Selling and Upselling:

CRM data can be leveraged to identify cross-selling and upselling opportunities, maximizing revenue from existing customers. For example, Amazon uses CRM data to recommend products based on customer purchase history, facilitating cross-selling and encouraging customers to make additional purchases.

Mobile CRM Accessibility:

Mobile CRM applications provide opportunities for businesses to access customer data on the go and enhance field sales and service operations. For example, Zoho CRM's mobile app allows sales representatives to access and update customer information, manage tasks, and track deals from their mobile devices.

Integration with Business Systems:

CRM integration with other business systems, such as ERP or marketing automation, streamlines operations and provides a unified view of business processes. For example, Microsoft Dynamics 365 integrates CRM and ERP functionalities, allowing businesses to manage customer relationships and business operations seamlessly.

Social Media Engagement:

Integrating CRM with social media platforms enables businesses to engage with customers on social channels and gather valuable insights. For example, Salesforce Social Studio integrates with CRM, allowing businesses to monitor social media conversations, engage with customers, and track social media interactions within the CRM platform.

ETHICAL ISSUES IN CRM (Nov., 2019; April, 2019)

Ethics in the context of Customer Relationship Management (CRM) refers to the principles and standards that guide the responsible and fair treatment of customers and their data. It involves conducting business in a manner that respects customer rights, ensures transparency, and prioritizes the well-being and privacy of individuals. Ethical considerations in CRM are crucial for building and maintaining trust, fostering positive relationships, and complying with legal and regulatory requirements. The main ethical issues in CRM:

Customer Privacy:

Respecting and safeguarding the privacy of customer data, ensuring it is collected, processed, and stored securely and used only for legitimate purposes. For example, obtaining explicit consent before collecting personal information and implementing robust security measures to protect customer data.

Transparency and Communication:

Providing clear and honest communication with customers about how their data will be used, what they can expect from the CRM system, and any changes to policies or practices. For example, maintaining transparent privacy policies and informing customers about data collection practices during interactions.

Informed Consent:

Obtaining informed and explicit consent from customers before collecting, processing, or sharing their personal information. For example, allowing customers to opt-in or opt-out of marketing communications and clearly explaining the purposes of data collection.

Fair and Responsible Use of Data:

Ensuring that CRM practices, including data analysis and decision-making, are fair, unbiased, and do not lead to discriminatory outcomes. For example, regularly auditing algorithms used in CRM to identify and rectify biases and ensuring that data-driven decisions are equitable.

Security and Data Protection:

Implementing robust security measures to protect customer data from unauthorized access, breaches, or misuse. For example, using encryption, access controls, and regular security audits to safeguard sensitive customer information within the CRM system.

Customer Empowerment:

Empowering customers by providing them with control over their data, allowing them to access, correct, or delete their information. For example, offering self-service options within the CRM system, enabling customers to manage their preferences and control the use of their data.

Trust-Building Practices:

Building and maintaining trust with customers through reliable services, transparent communication, and ethical business practices. For example, resolving customer issues promptly, being transparent about business operations, and delivering on promises made to customers.

Fair Marketing Practices:

Engaging in marketing practices that are truthful, transparent, and respectful of customer choices. For example, avoiding deceptive marketing tactics, clearly stating terms and conditions, and providing accurate information about products or services.

Compliance with Regulations:

Adhering to legal and regulatory requirements related to data protection, privacy, and consumer rights. For example, complying with international regulations like GDPR, HIPAA, or other local data protection laws relevant to the business and its customers.

Continuous Improvement:

Customer Relationship Management

Committing to continuous improvement in CRM practices, incorporating feedback, and adapting to evolving ethical standards. For example, regularly reviewing and updating privacy policies, security measures, and ethical guidelines to align with industry best practices.

QUESTIONS

Multiple Choice Questions:

(a) _____ provides access to all customer information including enquiry status and correspondence.
(i) Customer Management (ii) Knowledge management (iii) Account management (iv) Back end integration

(b) _____ access to customer information and history, allowing sales teams and customer service teams to function efficiently.
(i) Customer Management (ii) Knowledge management (iii) Account management (iv) Back end integration

(c) _____ also includes a response to a prospective customer immediately after the inquiry without any delay.
(i) Customer acquisition (ii) Customer satisfaction (iii) Customer retention (iv) E-CRM

(d) It is a well-established fact that the cost of acquiring a customer is _____ the cost of retaining an existing customer.
(i) Three times (ii) Four times (iii) Two times (iv) Five times

(e) _____ is a key element to E-CRM strategy.
(i) Customer acquisition (ii) Customer. win-back (iii) Customer retention (iv) E-CRM

(f) Calls from customers regarding their queries, problems, and suggestions are _____ calls. (Oct. 18)
(i) inbound (ii) outbound (iii) directional (iv) horizontal

Answers:- (a - i), (b - iii), (c - i), (d - iv), (e - ii), (f - i)

Fill in the blanks:

(a) ____ is an integrated online sale, marketing and service strategy that is used to identify, attract and retain an organization's customers.
(b) There are E's in E-CRM.
(c) _____ takes marketing techniques and concepts, and applies them through the electronic medium of the internet.
(d) E-CRM is an integrated online sales, marketing and service strategy that is used to identify, attract and retain an _____.
(e) _____ relates to codes of conduct regarded as right and good, based on morality or values, faith or some higher authority.
(f) CRM Solution providers are also working on providing simpler and easier ways of handling customer data using mobile devices which are known as _____.
(g) Key ethical issues in the information age, including the increased ubiquity of computerized databases, are often popularly summarized under the four headings of _____.

Answers:- (a) E-CRM, (b) Six, (c) E-Marketing, (d) Organization's customers, (e) Ethics, (f) Mobile CRM, (g) P-A-P-A (Privacy, Accuracy, Property, Accessibility)

Match the Following:-

Customer Relationship Management

Group 'A'	Group 'B'
(a) Customer management	i. Billing, inventory, and logistics
(b) Knowledge management	ii. Centralized knowledge base
(c) Account management	iii. Report generation
(d) Case management	iv. Handling customer information
(e) Back-end integration	v. Escalates priority cases
(f) Reporting and analysis	vi. Access to customer information

Answers:- (a-iv), (b-ii), (c-vi), (d-v), (e-i), (f-iii)

Long answer typed questions:

Q. Write a short note on 'inbound communication management'. (April, 2023; April, 2019)

Q. Write a short note on 'e-mail response management'. (April, 2023; Nov. 2022, Nov. 2019; Nov. 2018)

Q. Write a short note on 'e-CRM'. (April, 2023, Nov. 2022; Nov. 2019; April, 2019; Nov. 2018)

Q. Write a short note on mobile CRM (Nov. 2022; Nov. 2018)

Q. Write a short note on opportunities of CRM (Nov. 2022, Nov. 2019)

Q. Explain the software app for customer service (Nov. 2019)

Q. Write a short note on 'social networking and CRM' (April, 2023; Nov. 2019; April, 2019; Nov. 2018)

Q. Write down the ethical issues in CRM. (Nov. 2019; April, 2019)

Q. Write a short note on global CRM. (April, 2019)

Q. Discuss privacy issues in CRM and solution for the same. (Nov. 2022; Nov. 2018)

Q. Write a short note on CRM challenges. (Nov. 2018)

Q. Write a short note on 'queuing and routing'. (April, 2023)

MULTIPLE CHOICE QUESTIONS FOR PRACTICE:

1) Interruption Marketing refers to any marketing activity that _____ a viewer's attention.
   (a) Interrupts (b) Premise (c) Transact (d) Relate
2) Permission Marketing is the way to make _____ work effectively.
   (a) Interruption (b) Advertising (c) Transactional (d) Relationship
3) Transactional Marketing is a business strategy that focuses on _____ transactions.
   (a) Interruption (b) Permission (c) Single point of sale (d) Relationship
4) Relationship Marketing is a business strategy that seeks to establish long term relationship with its customers rather than focusing on _____ .
   (a) Single Strategy (b) Permission Marketing (c) Transactional Marketing (d) Single Transaction
5) _____ is the person who suggests buying product or service.
   (a) Influencer (b) Buyer (c) Initiator (d) Decision Maker
6) _____ is the person who will choose which product to buy.
   (a) Influencer (b) Buyer (c) Initiator (d) Decision Maker
7) _____ is the person whose point of view or advice will influence the buying decision.
   (a) Influencer (b) Buyer (c) Initiator (d) Decision Maker
8) Quick response, efficient customer response, JIT are the techniques used for reducing _____ levels.
   (a) Price (b) Inflation (c) Stock (d) Customer
9) _____ refers to the Cumulative image of a product held by the consumer, resulting from long exposure to the product or marketing of the product.
   (a) Customer Category (b) Category Management (c) Communication d) Customer Franchise
10) Uncertain waits are longer than known _____ waits

(a) Certain (b) Long, (c) Finite (d) Infinite
11) _____ waits are longer than equitable waits
    (a) Longer (b) Unfair (c) Fair (d) Infinite
12) _____ waits are longer than explained waits
    (a) Unexplained (b) Equitable (c) Fair (d) Infinite
13) Unoccupied time feels _____ than occupied time.
    (a) longer (b) Shorter (c) Finite (d) Infinite
14) The flat part of curve in the middle of the diagram reflecting link between customer satisfaction and retention is called as _____.
    (a) Zone of Retention (b) Zone of CRM (c) Zone of Indifference (d) Zone of difference
15) Artificial neural networks, Genetic Algorithms, decision trees are commonly used tools of _____.
    (a) Data Interpretation (b) Data Mining (c) Data retrieving (d) Data Analysis
16) _____ analysis operates at the server level by collecting clickstream data related to the path the user takes when navigating through the site.
    (a) Data (b) Mining (c) Traffic (d) E-commerce
17) _____ based analysis uses clickstream data to determine the effectiveness of the site as a channel to-market quantifying the users' behavior while on the web site.
    (a) Data (b) Mining (c) Traffic (d) E-commerce
18) Administrators can define _____ for each user by setting the design of the portal structure for different users.
    (a) Branding (b) Marketing (c) Advertising (d) Personalization
19) _____ refers to as extremely unsatisfied Customer
    (a) Detectors (b) Rejecters (c) Vulnerable (d) Terrorists
20) _____ can be practiced by adoption of new products and services.
    (a) Cross Selling (b) Customer Retention (c) Customer Expansion (d) Up selling
21) _____ has a greater impact on retention than satisfaction.
    (a) Customer Category (b) Dissatisfaction (c) Communication (d) Customer Franchise
22) Customer _____ is a key element to CRM strategy.
    (a) Selling (b) Retention (c) Expansion (d) Win-back
23) _____ involves leveraging and building knowledge management architecture upon existing databases, data mining and data warehousing systems.
    (a) Evaluation (b) System analysis, design and development (c) Deployment (d) Win-back
24) Key ethical issues in the information age are often summarised under a headings with acronym P-A-P-A which stands for _____.
    (a) Privacy-Authencity-Property-Accessibility (b) Privacy-Accuracy-Propaganda-Accessibility (c) Privacy-Accuracy-Property-Alteration (d) Privacy-Accuracy-Property-Accessibility
25) The word _____ in B2B refer to electronic middlemen who are necessary to facilitate online trades between buyers and sellers which are both businesses.
    (a) Enterprises (b) intermediaries (c) Privacy (d) Customer
26) _____ is also known as opportunity management.
    (a) Customer relationship management (b) Lead management (c) Contact management (d) Knowledge management
27) _____ is a business statement that summarize why a customer should buy a particular product.
    (a) Customer relationship management (b) Customer Lifetime Value (c) Contact management (d) Knowledge management

28) Quality = Customer's perception - _____.
   (a) Customer experimentation (b) Customer Lifetime Value (c) Customer management (d) Customer Expectation
29) The gap model is also known as the _____ of service quality.
   (a) 3 Gaps Model (b) 2 Gaps Model (c) 5 Gaps Model (d) 6 Gaps Model
30) Expectations-Disconfirmation model suggests that if _____ perceive their expectations to be met, they are satisfied.
   (a) Manufacturers (b) Producers (/ Customers (d) B2B
31) The _____ gap indicates the difference between the service expected by customers and the service they receive
   (a) Service Delivery (b) Service quality (c) Service quantity (d) Service Productivity
32) _____ is an unpleasant fulfilment response.
   (a) Disqualification (b) Disappointment (c) Dissatisfaction (d) Satisfaction
33) As per walker loyalty Matrix, _____ customers have all the goals of continuing to do business with the company and they have a positive attitude towards this company.
   (a) Truly Loyal (b) Accessible (c) High risk (d) Trapped
34) As per walker loyalty Matrix, _____ customers have a good attitude about working with this company, but do not plan to continue their relationship.
   (a) Truly Loyal (b) Accessible (c) High risk (d) Trapped
35) As per walker loyalty Matrix, _____ customers show every sign of continuing business with you, but they're not very happy about it.
   (a) Truly Loyal (b) Accessible (c) High risk (d) Trapped
36) _____ customers are halfway out the door and not only will they no longer be a customer, but will also talk poorly about the company in the marketplace.
   (a) Truly Loyal (b) Accessible (c) High risk (d) Trapped
37) _____ is an integrated online sale, marketing and service strategy that is used to identify, attract and retain an organization's customers.
   (a) CRM (b) Customer Loyalty, (c) E-CRM (d) TRP
38) _____ CRM, the customer are many retail outlets loyalty programs can participate through individual mobile phones.
   (a) Mobile (b) Customer Loyalty (c) E-CRM (d) TRP
39) _____ is the study of how individuals, groups and organizations select, buy, use and dispose off goods, services, ideas or experiences to satisfy their needs and wants.
   (a) Consumer behavior (b) Product cycle (c) Purchase behavior (d) None of the above
40) Percentage or number of customers who move from one level to next level in buying decision process is called _____.
   (a) Conversion rates (b) Marketing rates (c) Shopping rates (d) Loyalty rates
41) The real value of a company's marketing research and information system lies in the _____.
   (a) Amount of data it generates (b) Marketing information system it follows (c) Variety of contact methods it uses (d) Quality of customer insights it provides
42) In CRM, findings about customers discovered through _____ techniques often lead to marketing opportunities.
   (a) Data warehouse (b) Customer loyalty management (c) Customer relationship strategy (d) Data mining
43) _____ are issued to key customers which transmits all the relevant information, details of previous and repeat purchases, to make it convenient for the customers to recall and for the banks to keep a track of the behavioural and purchase trends.
   (a) Customer card (b) Customer ATM card (c) Customer Credit card (d) Customer Smart card

Customer Relationship Management

44) A _____ is a professional who works either directly with or directly for the customers and prospective customers of a given company.
(a) Customer executive (b) Customer Complainant (c) Manager (d) Customer Service Representative

45) _____ are the most critical asset in a call centre as it is they who deliver the business performance.
(a) Location (b) People (e) Customer (d) Process

46) _____ technique is used to develop and use customer data to check their profile, retention and loyalty patterns.
(a) Data Operating (b) Data Warehousing and data mining (c) Data analysis (d) Data Interpretation

47) The process of forecasting contact centre workload and then scheduling agents to handle the workload is known as _____.
(a) CRM (b) Call scripting (c) Workforce management (d) Relationship marketing management

48) McDonald's has a strategy where a salesperson will ask for "Anything else would u like to order with French Fries?" It's a case of _____.
(a) Cross-Selling (b) Up-selling (c) Sales (d) Customer Satisfaction

49) Syndicate bank now caters to the needs of its customers by offering various ICICI prudential Mutual Fund schemes and help in strengthening the existing relationship with the Bank's clientele base. This strategy is known as _____.
(a) Cross-Selling (b) Up-selling (c) Sales (d) Customer Satisfaction

50) _____ is crucial to maintain and grow customer relationships to sustain profitable growth.
(a) Customer Management (b) Customer Retention (c) Customer Acquisition (d) Customer Attrition

Answers:-

1	a	11	b	21	b	31	b	41	d
2	b	12	a	22	d	32	c	42	d
3	c	13	a	23	a	33	a	43	d
4	d	14	c	24	d	34	b	44	d
5	c	15	b	25	b	35	d	45	c
6	d	16	c	26	b	36	c	46	b
7	a	17	d	27	b	37	c	47	c
8	c	18	d	28	d	38	a	48	a
9	d	19	d	29	c	39	a	49	a
10	c	20	c	30	c	40	a	50	d

UNIVERSITY QUESTION PAPER (SOLVED)

APRIL-2023

Q.1 A) Multiple choice questions: - Attempt any eight questions. (8)

i) Implementation of CRM involves _____ cost.
a) **high** b) low c) medium d) none

ii) _____ is included in the elements of service level agreement.
a) Accountability b) performance (c) remuneration d) **All of above**

iii) Selling high end version of a product is a part of
a) cross-selling b) **upselling** c) both a & b d) none

iv) Collective handling of letters, faxes and e-mails at one location is known as
a) call b) **contact** c) Cyber d) CRM

v) _____ is a strategy for winning back the customers
a) branding b) **rebranding** c) call scripting d) call routing

vi) Service quality can be measured through _____
a) tangibles b) empathy c) assurance d) **all of the above**

vii) _____ involves planning and organizing a service technician's activity plan for a particular time period.
a) critical path method (CPM) b) routing c) **scheduling** d) none.

viii) _____ management enables the service staff to review their workload, schedule, and priorities as directed by their manager & report back about the progress of issue resolution.
a) **activity** b) agency. c) assignment d) all of above

ix) _____ is a strategic application of processes & practices for managing relationships between customers and organizations operating in multiple countries.
a) social CRM b) mobile CRM c) **global CRM** d) e-CRM

x) _____ is extremely volatile & time sensitive as well.
a) collaborative data b) master data c) **transaction data** d) reference data

B) State whether the given statements are true or false. Attempt any seven. (7)

i) Customer retention helps to connect a new customer to the manager or person who can best assist them with their existing problem. **T**

ii) Personalization is a method of recommending products or services to visitors on the website. **T**

iii) Order tracking product configuration is a customer-centered service. **T**

iv) Customer gap is the gap between customer expectation and satisfaction. **T**

v) Location based routing means transferring the all to the most skilled agent. **T**

(vi) Dashboards may include data from various data sources and are fairly static. **F**

vii) Forecasting of workload & required staff is a part of work force analysis. **T**

viii) E-CRM makes it possible for the customer to connect with an organization with the click of a button. **T**

ix) CRM helps an organization by providing information related to its prospective & existing customers. **T**

x) SFA is an application of several digital & wireless technologies for supporting the activities of salesperson. **T**

Q.2

a) Define CRM. Explain the components and evolution of customer relationships.
b) "An organization can perform brand building using relationship marketing "-comment

OR

c) Explain the challenges and barriers in implementing CRM.
d) Write a note on service level agreement.

Q.3

a) Explain the concepts: i) call scripting   ii) behaviour prediction
b) Describe the types of data analysis.

OR

c) Explain the concepts: i) data reporting i) event based marketing
d) What are the quality issues identified in the data?

Q.4

a) What is customer value? Explain sales force
b) Discuss in detail planning and implementation of CRM.

(OR)

Q4 c) Explain the company profit chain.
   d) Discuss the strategies to fill the service gaps.

Q.5 **Nestle: Helping to Develop Local Dairy Industry**

Nestlé's dairy development heritage in India began humbly in Moga on 15 November 1961, collecting only 511 kgs of milk on our first day. Today Nestlé's Moga factory collects over 1.3 million kgs of milk per day during the flush season, with over 110,000 farmers in India selling milk to Nestlé. Nestlé's milk collection area has expanded over the years and today covers 30,000 square kilometres. We have also constructed 2,815 milk collection centres in villages across the country to facilitate our considerable daily milk collection.

One of Nestlé's many success stories in the dairy sector is that of milk farmer Jagdeep Singh Sandhu, who hails from the village Assal in Ferozepur. Jagdeep began dairy farming in 2001 with one buffalo as be found the milk market remunerative. By 2004, he had managed to gradually increase his herd of buffaloes to 25. He soon associated himself with Nestlé who, by 2007, had assisted him in procuring a loan and encouraged him to increase his cow herd to 36 animals. In 2008, Nestlé sponsored Jagdeep's visit to the World Dairy Exposition in USA to gain more knowledge regarding commercial dairy Tarming. After his visit, Nestlé introduced best practices for dairy farming at his farm, including better calf management, silage preparation and thed expansion. With the adaptation of best practices at Jagdeep's farm, he soon saw increased milk productivity. Nestlé consequently installed a milk chilling facility at his farm to ensure 'chilling at source'. In 2010, we also installed a milking parlour at his farm. Today Jagdeep owns 78 cow's dh all, with 40 cows in milk, producing an average of 700 kgs of milk daily. His total income from milk is INR 32, 00,000 every year. In his six-year long relationship with Nestlé, Jagdeep has come a long way and is today a role model for other farmers in the area. In September 2010, the Deputy Commissioner of Ferozepur visited Jagdeep's farm and highly commended his efforts.

Questions: 1. Has nestle succeeded in changing business through CRM?

2. State your observations regarding CRM in the case.

Customer Relationship Management

(OR)

C) Write short notes on: - (any 3)

1. Social CRM
2. Inbound communication management
3. E-mail response management
4. Queuing and routing
5. Features of e-CRM

Answer of Q.5 (Case Study)

Q1: Has Nestle succeeded in changing the business through CRM?

Yes, Nestle has succeeded in changing its business through Customer Relationship Management (CRM). The case study highlights several ways in which Nestle has effectively utilized CRM to transform its dairy business in India:

Expansion of Milk Collection: Nestle started with humble beginnings, collecting only 511 kgs of milk on the first day. Through CRM efforts, Nestle expanded its milk collection significantly. Today, it collects over 1.3 million kgs of milk per day, involving more than 1,10,000 farmers. This expansion indicates that Nestle has successfully built and maintained relationships with a vast network of dairy farmers.

Support for Farmers: Nestle's CRM strategy includes providing support and assistance to individual farmers like Jagdeep Singh Sandhu. Nestle assisted him in procuring a loan, sponsored his visit to the World Dairy Exposition in the USA, and introduced best practices for dairy farming on his farm. These actions demonstrate a strong commitment to nurturing long-term relationships with farmers, helping them improve their livelihoods.

Knowledge Sharing: Nestle's initiative to send Jagdeep to the World Dairy Exposition and subsequently introducing best practices at his farm showcases the sharing of knowledge and expertise. This knowledge transfer is a key aspect of CRM, as it helps in building trust and loyalty among farmers.

Technology Integration: Nestle's installation of a milk chilling facility and a milking parlor at Jagdeep's farm demonstrates its commitment to technological advancements and efficiency. This investment not only benefits the farmer but also ensures a consistent supply of high-quality milk for Nestle's operations.

Economic Impact: The case study highlights the substantial increase in Jagdeep's income, which is a result of Nestle's CRM efforts. This financial improvement for farmers is a clear indicator of Nestle's success in creating mutually beneficial relationships through CRM.

Recognition and Commendation: The visit of the Deputy Commissioner of Ferozpur to Jagdeep's farm and the commendation of his efforts further emphasize the positive impact Nestle has had on the local dairy industry, which reflects the success of its CRM approach.

Overall, Nestle's CRM efforts have not only changed its business but have also contributed significantly to the development of the local dairy industry by empowering individual farmers and creating a mutually beneficial ecosystem.

Q2: State your observations regarding CRM in the case.

Observations regarding CRM in the case include:

Customer-Centric Approach: Nestle's CRM strategy is strongly customer-centric, focusing on building and maintaining relationships with individual dairy farmers. This approach is evident through personalized support, knowledge sharing, and technology integration to improve the farmers' livelihoods.

Long-Term Relationship Building: Nestle's commitment to farmers' long-term success is a key CRM observation. The company goes beyond just purchasing milk; it invests in the farmers' growth and development, thereby ensuring their loyalty and continued partnership.

Knowledge Transfer: Nestle's emphasis on knowledge transfer through initiatives like sponsoring Jagdeep's visit to the World Dairy Exposition and introducing best practices demonstrates its dedication to sharing expertise and helping farmers improve their dairy operations.

Technology Adoption: CRM in this case also involves technological advancements, such as installing milk chilling facilities and milking parlors. These investments enhance efficiency and product quality while benefiting the farmers.

Economic Impact: A significant observation is the positive economic impact of Nestle's CRM efforts. The increase in farmers' income reflects the success of the company's strategy in improving their lives and livelihoods.

Recognition and Reputation: Nestle's CRM efforts have led to recognition and commendation from local authorities, showcasing the positive reputation and impact the company has created in the local dairy industry.

NOVEMBER-2022

Q.1 A) Multiple choice questions: - Attempt any eight questions. (8)

1. A buyer who yields revenue which exceeds by an acceptable amount of cost is called as a _____ customer. (Loyal, integral, **profitable**, none)
2. Technology, process and people are the pillars of _____ management. (**Knowledge**, Lead, Contact, None)
3. Collective handling of letters, faxes and e-mails at one location is known as a _____ center. (call, **contact**, inbound, none)
4. Customer Gap is a gap between customer expectation and _____ .(**perception**, satisfaction, loyalty, none)
5. Order tracking, product configuration is a _____ centered service. (**customer**, producer, wholesaler, retailer)
6. _____ are the elements of SLA. (Accountability, Performance, Remuneration, **All of the Above**)
7. _____ based routing routes incoming calls based on the customers location. (**location**, performance, skills, least occupied)
8. _____ is the heart of selling process. (Customer delight, **customer satisfaction**, customer retention, customer loyalty)
9. The act to changing one brand of product to other is called as _____. (Brand Equity, **Brand Switching**, Brand Loyalty, None)
10. _____ involves planning and organizing a service technician's activity plan for a particular time period. (Queuing, Routing, **Scheduling**, None)

B) State whether True or False. Attempt any seven. (7)

1. Social networking helps to connect with new prospects. **T**
2. Forecasting of workload and required staff is part of workforce analysis. **T**

3. CVM model creates value for customers by providing superior quality products at affordable prices. **F**

4. E-CRM provides a centralized knowledge base that handles and shares customer information. **T**

5. Language is a barrier for effective implementation of global CRM. **T**

6. Warehouse data describes business event. **F**

7. Customer value is a function of cash flow, profitability and customer service. **T**

8. The SLA should include a detailed description of various services. **T**

9. Traffic analysis and e-commerce analysis are the two levels of click-stream analysis. **T**

10. Relationship marketing is cross-functional marketing. **T**

Q2.
- a) Explain the benefits of CRM to customers as well as organizations. (8)
- b) Define CRM, Explain its objectives. (7)

OR
- c) Explain Service Level agreement? Explain its elements? (8)
- d) What do you mean by CRM? Explain types of CRM? (7)

Q3.
- a) What do you mean by brand switching? Discuss the reasons for the same. (8)
- b) Explain components of call centres. (7)

OR
- c) Explain Customer retention, write in detail about the need for customer retention? (8)
- d) Write in detail about the types of data analysis? (7)

Q4.
- a) Explain service gap model. (8)
- b) What are the objectives of CRM strategy? (7)

OR
- c) Discuss the strategies to fill the service gaps. (8)
- d) Explain CRM strategy cycle. (7)

Q5. a) Elaborate the recent trends in CRM (8)
  b) Discuss the privacy issues in CRM and solutions for the same. (7)

OR

C) Short Notes (Any 3) (15)

1. Benefits of E-CRM

2. Contract Management.

3. Opportunities for CRM

Customer Relationship Management

4. Email Response Management System

5. Steps in Implementation of Mobile CRM.

November-2019

Q.1 A) Multiple choice questions: - Attempt any eight questions. (8)

i) Long term CRM involves _____ operational cost.

a) **high** b) low c) medium d) none

ii) _____ means transferring the call to the available agent to reduce the waiting time of the customers.

    a) **Call routing** b) call scripting c) personalization d) channel optimization

iii) _____ is an act of selling additional products to customers.

    a) **Cross-selling** b) up-selling c) both a & b d) none

iv) _____ is a method of recommending products or services to customers on websites.

    a) Clickstream analysis b) online analytical process c) **collaborative filtering** d) traffic analysis

v) A service level agreement (SLA) is a tool for building relationship with high value customers.
a) **formal** b) informal c) shared d) none
vi) ____ is the heart of selling process.
a) customer delight b) **customer satisfaction** c) customer retention d) customer loyalty

vii) _____ is also known as opportunity management.
a) customer relationship management b) **lead management** c) contact management d) knowledge management
viii) Privacy laws protect the interest of ____.
a) Customers b) employees c) organizations d) **all**
ix) _____ relationship exists when a customer has tried a product for the first time.
a) acquaintance b) friend c) partner d) **stranger**
x) _____ are calculations or summaries of historical information that often compares trends over times.
a) **business view data** b) warehouse data c) transaction data d) reference data

Q.1. B) State whether the given statements are true or false- Attempt any seven. (7)

1) Win back is the first stage in the CRM strategy cycle. **F**
2) Cyber agents are viable means of providing basic customer support. **T**
3) Event based marketing is also known as trigger marketing. **T**
4) Calls made by customers to the call centers is a part of inbound communication. **T**

5) Service delivery gap is a communication gap. **F**
6) Customer value management (CVM) is also known as customer value added approach. **T**

7) CRM strategy focuses only on creation of valuable customers. **F**
8) E-CRM is derived from e-commerce. **T**
9) Cloud computing software is efficient means for collecting customer data. **T**
10) CRM maintains relationships with customers by frequent contacts so as to obtain their maximum data. **F**

(2) (a) Explain SLA and main elements of good SLA. (8)
(b) Explain the challenges and barriers in implementing CRM. (7)
OR
(c) Write a note on Service level Agreement. (8)
(d) Define CRM and explain its components in detail. (7)
(3) (a) What is Data Management? Discuss different types of Data. (8)
(b) Discuss Customer Profitability and value Modelling. (7)
OR
(c) What are the quality issues identified in the data. (8)
(d) Explain customer retention and methods to improve customer retention. (7)
(4) (a) Write in detail the steps for implementing a CRM program. (8)
(b) What are the complexities of CRM strategy. (7)
OR
(c) Explain CRM Strategy Cycle. (8)
(d) Explain the concept of Knowledge Management. (7)
(5) (a) Explain the features of E-CRM. (8)
(b) Explain the software App for Customer Service. (7)
OR
(c) Write short notes on the following: (Any Three) (15)
(1) Email response system. (2) Social Networking and CRM. (3) Levels of E-CRM. (4) Ethical Issues in CRM. (5) Recent trends in CRM.

MAY-2019

Q1 (A) Multiple choice questions: Attempt any eight questions. (8)

1. A business strategy designed to optimise profitability, revenue and _____ satisfaction.
a. Producer b. distributor c. **consumer** d. government.

2. CRM Is a discipline that covers all _____ needed to build strong relationships with customers
a. Essential b. **elements** c. equipment's d. endeavours

3. Customer relationship management saves expensive data and ____ time.
a. Membership b. **management** c. movements d. none of these

4. The ____ tier describes the company's most profitable customers.
a. Gold b. **platinum** c. iron d. lead

5. CRM and relationship marketing focus on customer retention and _____.
a. Mutuality b. **loyalty** c) treaty d. popularity

6. Cross - selling done correctly means _____ the right product to the right customer.

a. Producing b. marketing c. **selling** d. campaigning

7. Event based marketing is a _____ sensitive marketing.
a) Price b) place c) **time** d) value

8) _____ event-based marketing means reaching to a customer event in optimal time frame.
a) Static b) **dynamic** c) general d) special

9) Data _____ is the process of collecting and submitting data to the entitled authorities.
a) Assembling b recording c) **reporting** d) reversing

10. OLAP means the online _____ processing.
a) **Analytical** b) administrative c adjustment d) affiliation

B) State whether the following statements are true or false.
1) CRM is needed in B2B transactions. **T**
2) Call routing helps to save expensive man hours. **T**
3) Usually the information is the raw material of CRM. **T**
4) Customers evolve from strangers to partners. **T**
5) Profitability is a piece of the total revenue puzzle. **T**
6) CRM wastes the time and money of service organisation. **F**
7) Customer segmentation refers to categories the products for the customer. **F**
8) Call centres offer a range of services like all night convenience stores for 12 hours. **F**
9) Listening, responding and improving does not help in customer care. **F**
10) The credit card may result in reducing the customer's monthly shopping trips. **T**

2) (a) Explain the evolution of customer relationships. (8)
(b) What are the objectives of CRM? (7)
OR
(c) What are the components of CRM? (8)
(d) Explain customer profitability segments. (7)
(3) (a) Explain the types of data analysis. (8)
(b) Explain planning and getting information quality. (7)
OR
(c) Explain the concepts of cross-selling and up-selling. (8)
(d) Explain identifying data quality issues. (7)
(4) (a) Bring out the relevance of 3E in CRM. (8)
(b) State and explain the steps involved in implementation of CRM. (7)
OR
(c) Explain the CRM strategy cycle. (8)
(d) Explain sales force automation with suitable examples. (7)
(5) (a) Explain the ethical issues in CRM. (8)
(b) UberEATS has been launched in the US for quite some time now. And they are expanding at a fast pace in India. Food delivery is a multi- billion-dollar business and Uber definitely wants a share of the pie. Coupled with its tech-backing and sophisticated optimization algorithms its trying its best to crack this market. Swiggy will prove to be a tough competitor, given its massive base already, and a solid delivery network. But UberEATS is going to try all tricks up its sleeve to woo the restaurants and the customers and

be the market leader in the country. Uber wants to have riders listed on the platform to take care of the deliver. They are trying to create a true 3-way marketplace for this business: The restaurants, delivery partners and the end users (who order the meals). This is a tough problem to crack, but it is Uber after all. How can social media CRM strategies be used in case of UberEATS? (7)

OR

(c) Write short notes on: (Any Three) (15)
(1) Global CRM. (2) Social networking and CRM. (3) Benefits of E- CRM. (4) Different levels of E-CRM. (5) Inbound and outbound communication management.

Answer of Q. 5 (a)
Answer
Social media and CRM (Customer Relationship Management) strategies can play a crucial role in helping Uber Eats establish a strong presence and compete effectively in the food delivery market in India. Here are some ways these strategies can be used:

Customer Engagement and Feedback: Uber Eats can use social media platforms like Facebook, Twitter, Instagram, and others to engage with customers. They can encourage customers to share their experiences, reviews, and feedback about the service. This engagement can help in building a community of loyal customers and provide valuable insights for improving the platform.

Personalized Marketing: CRM can help Uber Eats analyze customer data to understand preferences, ordering habits, and demographics. With this information, they can create personalized marketing campaigns. For example, sending tailored promotions and recommendations to individual customers based on their past orders can boost customer retention and sales.

Promotions and Discounts: Uber Eats can leverage social media to run promotions and offer discounts to attract new customers and retain existing ones. Running exclusive social media campaigns with promo codes can create a buzz and drive more orders.

Responsive Customer Support: CRM systems can track customer interactions and issues, enabling Uber Eats to provide quick and efficient customer support. Social media can also serve as a channel for customers to reach out for support and receive timely responses.

Influencer Marketing: Collaborating with local food influencers and bloggers can help Uber Eats gain visibility and credibility in the market. These influencers can promote the platform through their social media channels and reviews.

User-Generated Content: Encourage customers to share their food photos and experiences on social media using a specific hashtag related to Uber Eats. This user-generated content can serve as free advertising and create a sense of community among users.

Targeted Advertising: Use CRM data to target specific customer segments with paid social media advertising. For instance, targeting ads to users who haven't ordered in a while with a special offer can help re-engage them.

Loyalty Programs: Implement a CRM-driven loyalty program that rewards frequent customers with discounts, free deliveries, or exclusive offers. Promote these programs through social media to attract and retain loyal customers.

Competitor Analysis: Monitor competitors, including Swiggy and others, on social media to understand their strategies and customer sentiment. This information can inform Uber Eats' own marketing and service improvement efforts.

Data Analytics: Continuously analyze data from CRM systems and social media to track the effectiveness of marketing campaigns, customer satisfaction, and trends in the market. Adjust strategies based on insights to stay competitive.

November-2018

Q.1 A) Multiple choice questions: - Attempt any eight questions. (8)

1. ____ is a component of CRM.
i) people ii) technology iii) Information iv) **all of the above**

2. Calls from customers regarding their queries, problems and suggestions are ___ calls.

i) **inbound** ii) outbound iii) directional iv) horizontal

3. Offering a greater quantity for a slightly higher price is an example of ____.
i) **cross selling** ii) upselling iii) personalization iv) bancassurance

4. ____exists when perception > expectation.
i) customer satisfaction ii) customer dissatisfaction iii) **customer delight** iv) customer engagement

5. ____a central point in an enterprise from which all customer contacts are maintained such as e-mails, newsletters, chats etc.

i) call center ii) **contact center** iii) customer care center [v] development center

6. ____is a method of recommending products or services to visitors on websites.
i) clickstream analysis. ii) online analytical process iii) **collaborative filtering** iv) traffic analysis

7. The process of forecasting contact center workloads and then scheduling agents to handle the workload is known as ____.
i) CRM ii) call scripting iii) **workforce management** iv) relationship marketing management

8. ____ is a business statement that summarizes why a customer should buy a particular product.

i) **customer value proposition** ii) customer lifetime value iii) customer care value iv) company profit chain

9. ERP stands for ____.

a) employee resource planning b) employee relationship planning c) entrepreneur resource planning d) **enterprise resource planning**

10. Company 3E measure does not include ____.

a) effectiveness ii) **endurance** iii) employee change iv) efficiency

Customer Relationship Management

B) State whether the statements are true or false. Attempt any seven. (7)

1. Customer relationship agreement is a contract between a service provider and the end user that defines the level of service expected from the service provider. **T**
2. Personalization consists of tailoring a service or product to accommodate specific individual needs. **T**
3. Customer engagement is not a customer retention strategy. **F**
4. Data reporting is a written script that has correct wordings and assist an agent in handing a contact. **F**
5. Event based marketing is also known as trigger marketing. **T**
6. Data profiling helps to plan and get qualitative information **T**.
7. Customer lifetime value (CLV) is the result of cumulative net returns received over the lifetime of customers. **T**
8. Customer retention is the first step in CRM strategy cycle. **F**

9. Service quality gap indicates the difference between the service expected by customers and the service they actually receive. **T**

10. Sales force automation involves converting manual sales activities to electronic processes through the use of various combinations of hardware and software applications. **T**

Q.2 a) Define CRM. Explain the different profitability segments. (8)

b) Write a note on service level agreement. (7)

OR

a) What is relationship marketing management? Explain various relationship development strategies. (8)

b) Briefly explain the different barriers in implementing effective CRM. (7)

Q.3 a) Explain the different types of data. (8)

b) What is call routing? Explain the different types of routing techniques. (7)

OR

a) Discuss the customer profitability and value modelling. (8)

b) Explain the concepts of event-based marketing and web-based self-service. (7)

Q.4 a) Explain the concept of knowledge management. (8)

b) Explain 828 and sales in CRM. (7)

OR

c) Describe the steps involved in implementation of CRM. (8)

d) Discuss the objectives of CRM strategy. (7)

Customer Relationship Management

Q.5 a) Discuss the privacy issues in CRM and the solution for the same.

b) Aakash LTD was the oldest financial service organization in Bhopal. Over the years there was rapid Increase in the customer base. However, it was still using traditional marketing tools like word of mouth publicity and the communication channels were not very effective. The organization was facing difficulty in maintaining customer database and managing relationships with customers. Although the marketing team of the organization left no stone unturned for persuading customers by providing them huge discount on product and services but it was not fruitful. This resulted in huge loss.
As a consultant suggest remedial measures to rectify the situation.

OR

c) Write short notes on any 3

1. Mobile CRM
2. E-mail response management system.
3. Levels of CRM.
4. CRM challenges.
5. Social networking and CRM.

Answer of Q. 5 (b)

To rectify the situation at Aakash Ltd, the organization should consider implementing a comprehensive strategy that modernizes its marketing and customer relationship management efforts. Here are some remedial measures to consider:

Digital Transformation:

Invest in a robust Customer Relationship Management (CRM) system to effectively manage customer data, preferences, and interactions.

Develop a user-friendly website and mobile app for customers to access services, view products, and make inquiries.

Embrace digital marketing strategies such as email marketing, social media advertising, and search engine optimization (SEO) to reach a wider audience.

Customer Segmentation:

Segment the customer base to understand their diverse needs and preferences. This will enable targeted marketing and personalized offers.

Data Analytics:

Utilize data analytics tools to gain insights into customer behavior and preferences. This data can guide marketing and product/service development efforts.

Effective Communication:

Establish clear and consistent communication channels with customers, such as email newsletters, SMS alerts, and social media updates.

Implement a responsive customer support system to address inquiries and complaints promptly.

Customer Loyalty Programs:

Design and implement loyalty programs that reward repeat customers and incentivize them to stay loyal to Aakash Ltd.

Referral Programs:

Encourage satisfied customers to refer friends and family by offering referral rewards. Word of mouth can still be valuable if managed systematically.

Streamline Discounts and Promotions:

Evaluate the effectiveness of discounts and promotions. Consider offering targeted discounts based on customer behavior and preferences rather than blanket discounts.

Employee Training:

Train employees in customer service excellence, ensuring they understand the importance of building and maintaining strong customer relationships.

Feedback Mechanisms:

Implement feedback mechanisms like surveys and reviews to gather customer opinions and suggestions for improvement.

Market Research:

Conduct market research to understand changing customer trends, competitive landscape, and emerging opportunities.

Strategic Partnerships:

Explore partnerships with other businesses or financial service providers to enhance the range of services offered.

Budget Reallocation:

Reallocate marketing budgets from traditional methods towards digital marketing and customer engagement strategies.

Performance Metrics:

Establish key performance indicators (KPIs) to measure the success of marketing and customer relationship efforts. Regularly review and adjust strategies based on these metrics.

Compliance and Data Security:

Ensure strict compliance with data protection regulations (e.g., GDPR) to safeguard customer information and build trust.

www.ingramcontent.com/pod-product-compliance
Lightning Source LLC
Chambersburg PA
CBHW062106220526
45471CB00010B/3620